GET THAT FREAK

GET THAT FREAK

Homophobia and Transphobia in High Schools

Rebecca Haskell & Brian Burtch

Fernwood Publishing • Halifax & Winnipeg

Editing: Elizabeth Phinney
Cover design: John van der Woude
Text design: Brenda Conroy
Printed and bound in Canada by Hignell Book Printing

Published in Canada by Fernwood Publishing
32 Oceanvista Lane
Black Point, Nova Scotia, B0J 1B0
and 748 Broadway Avenue, Winnipeg, Manitoba, R3G 0X3
www.fernwoodpublishing.ca

Fernwood Publishing Company Limited gratefully acknowledges the financial support of the Government of Canada through the Canada Book Fund, the Canada Council for the Arts, the Nova Scotia Department of Tourism and Culture and the Province of Manitoba, through the Book Publishing Tax Credit, for our publishing program.

Library and Archives Canada Cataloguing in Publication

Haskell, Rebecca
Get that freak: homophobia and transphobia in high schools / Rebecca Haskell, Brian Burtch.

(Basics)
Includes bibliographical references.
ISBN 978-1-55266-378-3

1. Bullying in schools—British Columbia. 2. Homophobia in high schools—British Columbia. 3. Gay high school students—British Columbia. 4. Bullying in schools—British Columbia—Prevention. I. Burtch, Brian E., 1949– II. Title. III. Series: Fernwood basics.

LB3013.34.C3H38 2010   371.5'809711   C2010-902862-7

Contents

Acknowledgements 8

Glossary 9

Introduction The Hidden Curriculum of Bullying 11
    Terminology 12
    About Our Study 14

1   Homophobia and Transphobia in Schools 19
    Prevalence of Homophobic Bullying 27
    Prevalence of Transphobic Bullying 30

2   Experiences of HTP in High School 35
    Physical Harassment 35
    Subtle Harassment 40
    Resistance to HTP 53
    Positive High-School Experiences 55

3   Outcomes and Origins of HTP 59
    Effects of HTP Bullying in High School 59
    Rooting Out HTP: Origins and Implications 69

4   A Gentle Violence? 89
    Michel Foucault and Pierre Bourdieu: A Brief Introduction 90
    From the "Spectacle" of Physical Violence to "Gentle Violence" 92
    Creating Docile Bodies 96
    Pushing Back against Oppression in School 99
    Explaining HTP 101
    Lack of Information and Misinformation 104
    Reducing HTP: Outing HTP Bullying 106
    Research As Resistance 108

Conclusion "A Better Place" 111

References 115

For queer youth who experience bullying in school and whose resilience is an inspiration, and for everyone who works to reduce harassment toward queer youth. —R.H. and B.B.

For Joe Thomas (Joey) and my family (biological and chosen) for loving and supporting me. R.H.

For Carol Hird and Bernard Motut —B.B.

Acknowledgements

We are grateful to the sixteen young adults who shared their experiences of high-school bullying and to the approximately thirty undergraduate Criminology students who contributed to an earlier pilot project during Rebecca's coursework for her master's degree. We thank Alice Hartley, who kindly arranged a meeting room at Simon Fraser University's (SFU) downtown campus. We are indebted to staff in SFU's School of Criminology. Marie Krbavac helped with computer-related problems. And we appreciate the feedback received from Dr. Jacqueline Faubert and Dr. Helen Leung.

We are also grateful to the Vancouver Pride Society, who provided funding through their Legacy Fund grant in support of initiatives for lesbian, gay, bisexual and trans (LGBT) communities in Vancouver.

A thank-you is extended to Kris Wells, Tanya Callaghan, Gerald Walton, Liz Meyer and Don Cochrane for their inspiration and support. We also gratefully acknowledge people who provided input and spread the word about the study, including Tim Timberg and barbara findlay.

We are very grateful to the staff at Fernwood Publishing, especially to Errol Sharpe, who took the time to meet with us, and to Candida Hadley for her helpful insights.

Thanks to Rebecca's "study buddies" (Telle, Meag, Mary, Chris, Shane and Andrew), who fuelled many productive days and nights.

Brian appreciates the ongoing support of his colleagues in the School of Criminology and the Department of Gender, Sexuality and Women's Studies at SFU. Loved ones have been a great support, with a special mention going to his wife, Carol Hird, and his fine friend Bernie Motut.

Glossary

Bisexual — Refers to an individual who is sexually attracted to both men and women.

Drag — Dressing/acting as the other gender for theatrical effect (Stewart 1995).

Gay — A term adopted in the twentieth century by lesbians and gay men to refer to themselves (Stewart 1995).

Gender variant — A synonym for transgender, used to describe people outside of the male-female framework (Serano 2007, 25).

Genderism — "The belief that there are, and should be, only two genders, and that one's gender, or most aspects of it, are inevitably tied to biological sex" (Trans Accessibility Project n.d., section titled "Genderism").

Genderqueer — Rooted in queer theory, a term meant to disrupt the binary male-female gender framework.

Heterosexism — Prejudice or bias in favour of heterosexuality as the norm over homosexuality. Usually refers to carelessness or thoughtlessness or automatic assumptions about the heterosexuality of others. Often heterosexism is conceived of as a precondition for homophobia (Stewart 1995).

Homophobia — The fear or hatred of homosexuality, based on assumptions about the naturalness of privileging heterosexuality. Usually used to describe discriminatory practices of actions against queer people (Stewart 1995).

Lesbian — Taken from the name of the island, Lesbos, that was home to the Greek poet Sappho. Refers to women romantically interested in other women.

Outing

The practice of publicizing people's LGBTTQ identity against their will (Stewart 1995).

Queer

The term "queer" is used to refer to any sexual or gender expressions or identities that do not conform to the heteronormative and either/or gender frameworks. The term is popular in queer theory, a relatively new branch of study emerging from feminist theories, gay and lesbian studies, and the work of constructionists such as Judith Butler, Michael Foucault and Eve Sedgwick (Klages 1997, para. 1). Queer theory helps us to deconstruct and confound normative categories of sexuality and gender by "presenting experiences... that challenge such binaries" (Kitzinger and Wilkinson 1994, 452).

Transgender

An umbrella term referring to individuals who identify themselves along the continuum of gender, but not as male or female. Sometimes used specifically to refer to people who do not wish to have sex reassignment surgery (Thompson 2004).

Transphobia

"A reaction of fear, loathing and discriminatory treatment of people whose gender identity or gender presentation — or *perceived gender or gender identity* — does not match in the socially accepted way, the sex they were assigned at birth. Transgender people, transsexuals and intersex people are most frequently the targets of transphobia." ("Glossary" 2009).

Transsexual

A medical term used to describe an individual who undergoes hormonal and surgical procedures to appear as the other sex than that assigned to them at birth. A transsexual male refers to someone who "transitioned" from female to male and a transsexual female to someone who transitioned from male to female (Forde 2006).

Two-Spirit

A term originally "used by North American Aboriginal societies to describe what Europeans now call Gay, Lesbian, Bisexual, Transgendered and Transsexual people" (Lerat 2004, 6).

The Hidden Curriculum of Bullying

> The struggle for true openness and intimacy is a lifelong struggle
> for all of us, gay and straight alike. And besides, a difficult life brings
> you to the core of yourself, where you learn what justice is and how
> it has been fought for. (Monette 1995, 204)

By the time children reach first grade, they are already familiar with what it means to be included or shunned, how it feels to be helped or to be hurt. Students in the early grades have already compiled a significant understanding — or misunderstanding — about what it means to be queer in a heterosexist society. Much of what they learned may be incorrect, born of fear and prejudice rather than factual information. As children grow into young adults these lessons intensify and are learned at home, in the media, and through interactions at school. Sometimes the lessons are brutal, involving bullying that is so persistent and hateful that young people take their own lives, whether they have been targeted for their sexual orientation, gender identity or any other number of reasons. At the time of writing this passage, the parents of a fifteen-year-old boy, Ashkan Sultani, were grieving his suicide, a death they attribute to the intense bullying he experienced at school (Bellaart 2010). The Sultanis are advocating for links to be made between bullying and suicide in suicide-prevention efforts of the Nanaimo-Ladysmith School District where their son attended school.

The Sultanis are among an increasing number of people who are recognizing schools as sites that produce and reproduce social hierarchies. For example, lesbian, gay, bisexual, trans, two-spirited and queer (LGBTTQ) identities are often denigrated. Students who claim these identities may be subjected to bullying behaviours that reinforce the "boundaries" of proper gender and sexual identity. But educators and students also have the potential to create an ethos of respect for queer people and to adopt a more radical, anti-oppressive approach in schools. El-Bushra (2000, 82) claims that the "institutions which shape the formulation of destructive identities can also be employed to shape constructive ones."

Enabling students to construct positive sexual and gender identities requires that transphobia and homophobia be acknowledged and addressed in the thick of conflict in high schools. Some argue that this is beginning to happen. In the past decade, increased attention has been given to bullying behaviours in schools. One needn't look any further than the daily news to see reports of student "swarmings" or vicious online bullying. School administrators and "experts" have devoted resources to enhance safe school policies and programs that have been implemented in the educational system (Walton 2004). Recently, school administrators, politicians, and the public in Canada have acknowledged that homophobic and, to a lesser extent, transphobic bullying is a concern in schools. That said, we also offer some evidence of a fairly leaden response or failure to respond to ongoing bullying, not only of queer students, but other students who may be easy targets for beatings, threats and shunning.

Relying on evidence of the prevalence of homophobic and transphobic (HTP) harassment among youth, we take as a given that HTP does happen in schools. The sixteen queer youth we spoke with shared retrospective accounts of experiences with HTP in British Columbia (B.C.) high schools. Their motivations for participating were to increase the visibility of queer youth in schools and to raise awareness about how even seemingly innocuous forms of HTP can manifest as a form of "gentle violence."

In keeping with feminist research principles espoused by Dorothy Smith (2005, 225), we treat the sixteen participants as the experts on their own lives and therefore of the HTP they experienced. This book is a venue for their voices, and they are presented throughout. Although research questions were devised before launching the focus groups and interviews, the themes that emerged and the recommendations made are a product of participants' experiences and the knowledge they shared with us.

Terminology

Definitions for the "queer vocabulary" used in this book are listed in the glossary preceding this section. As terms used throughout the book, however, a basic understanding of "homophobia" and "transphobia" would be beneficial. According to the *Routledge International Encyclopaedia of Queer Culture* (Forde 2006, 277), homophobia is "the fear or hatred of homosexuality" and is "based upon the assumption that homosexuality is unnatural or inferior to heterosexuality." Remarkably, the same encyclopedia does not include an entry on transphobia or gender bashing; Shelley (2008) notes how unfamiliar this term is to those in mainstream society. Parents, Families and Friends of Lesbians and Gays (PFLAG) Canada (Glossary 2009; emphasis in original) offers the following excellent definition of transphobia:

> [A] reaction of fear, loathing and discriminatory treatment of people whose gender identity or gender presentation — or *perceived gender or gender identity* — does not match in the socially accepted way, the sex they were assigned at birth. Transgender

people, transsexuals and intersex people are most frequently the targets of transphobia....

Several authors (Birden 2005; Redman 2000; Shelley 2008) believe that using the term "phobia" to explain harassment of LGBTTQ people "suggests a causal explanation for the subjugation of trans [and queer] lives, the thesis that transpeople incite — by their very existence and presence — *fear*" (Shelley 2008, 32; emphasis in original). These authors argue that using "phobia" implies that threats, putdowns and general harassment of queer people stem from individuals' psychological impairments, a focus that does not address societal and institutional roots. Because of the widespread knowledge of the term "homophobia" and its association with harassment of queer people, it is a term used throughout this work.

"Transphobia" is also a commonly used term in the trans community and this encouraged us to include it as well. For space considerations, we have shortened the phrase "homophobia and transphobia" or "homophobic and transphobic" to HTP in this book.

Distinguishing whether an interaction is evidence of transphobia or homophobia is often difficult, especially in a high-school environment where queer youth may not be "out." Even where youth are "out" as LGBTTQ, it can be difficult to assess motivations behind their harassment given the tendency to associate certain gendered behaviours and appearances with hetero- or homosexuality.

People often make stereotypical assumptions about one's sexuality based on gender expression. For example, females who engage in rough-and-tumble sports and who are outspoken are sometimes seen as masculine and perhaps suspected of being lesbians. Conversely, soft-spoken or artistically inclined males may be seen as effeminate and are often presumed to be gay. Gender plays a large role in what is often deemed homophobic harassment, and these events are not just about sexual orientation; discomfort with gender nonconformity is also likely a factor. To emphasize the importance of gender variance in incidents frequently labelled as homophobic, the term transphobia is adopted in this book. "Transphobia" is used broadly and applied to situations where gender variance or gender nonconformity (terms adopted from Wyss 2004) may have been an impetus for harassment. This was often the case for participants in this study.

Finally, the terms bullying and harassment are used interchangeably in this book. This project was not built on a preconceived definition of bullying, an approach that allowed participants' conceptualizations of bullying to be explored in the discussions. As Walton (2006, 11–12) points out, most research on bullying relies on a "generic conceptualisation" that focuses on "psychological motivations and the policing of behaviour, and thus do not address negative perceptions of difference that underlie incidents of bullying." For example, Olweus (1993, 9), a prominent scholar in the field of bullying, defines bullying as "repeated negative action towards a student or students." Negative actions include intentionally inflicting or attempting to inflict harm verbally or physically, or through social exclusion (Olweus 1993, 9). Walton (2006, 12), on the other hand, says that "the moments now widely known generically as bullying" reflect social anxieties about difference. Traditional conceptualizations, Walton (2006) contends, do not go far enough to acknowledge the normality of bullying nor the normalizing effects that bullying can have on others. As a form of social control, bullying works not only to devalue certain behaviours or appearances, but specific identities as well.

Whether HTP behaviours are termed bullying or harassment, they are not just sporadic incidents perpetrated by one or two "bad apples." HTP sentiments and their manifestations are the result of widespread heterosexism and rigid gender frameworks (genderism) in society. Indeed, participants in our study discussed how school environments mirror those in the larger society and contemplated how changes in B.C. high schools might effect change in the larger Canadian society.

About Our Study

Research from the U.S. (Kosciw, Diaz and Greytak 2008) and Canada (Egale Canada 2009) offers a glimpse into some contextual factors of HTP bullying: who are the bullies, who are the victims, how many people are involved as bystanders, how often bullying takes place, where it is likely to occur and how harm is manifested. To date, however, there has been an acute shortage of research exploring factors that lead to and characterize homophobic and transphobic harassment in Canadian high schools. We sought to close the gap in research by starting from the assumption that HTP does happen in high schools. Accordingly, we set out to explore experiences with these forms of harassment. Through interviews and discussion groups, we spoke with sixteen queer youth who had recently left a B.C. high school about their retrospective experiences with harassment based on sexual or gender identity in the school setting. Table 1.1 displays the gender identity and sexual orientation of each participant.

We asked each youth about the nature of homophobic and transphobic bullying (i.e., types of bullying, frequency, who was involved, location), and the effects the harassment had on them. Participants were asked to hypothesize about possible causes of HTP bullying and to suggest ways to prevent such bullying in high school. We also asked volunteers to share their positive experiences and outcomes. The weight of research on HTP rests on an assumption of bullying as a "social problem"; this study left room for more

Table 1.1 Demographics of Participants (N=16)

Gender Identity			
Female	Male	Gay/Androgynous	Left blank
3	8	3	2
Sexual Orientation			
Queer/Lesbian, Queer/Gay, Queer, Pansexual	Gay	Bisexual	Left blank
6	7	2	1

Note: Participants have been given pseudonyms to protect their identity. In the descriptions of participants in the quotes, an asterisk means that the young person did not identify either their gender identity or sexual orientation.

positive aspects linked with bullying and its aftermath. For instance, youth shared experiences in which they believed that school staff or classmates were accepting and supportive of their sexual or gender identities. When asked what came to mind when she first heard about the study, one young person said:

> For me, the first thing I thought of was a teacher that I had… he was openly gay…. It was his idea to found our school's GSA, I was the founding member. He was so supportive, he was always there to listen, he was always there to back me up on anything, so I just thought of him, like just the support that he provided for me in high school. (Phoenix, queer, androgynous)

As researchers, we struggled with how to convey our findings and use key theoretical concepts without the excessive use of jargon. Writing in a clear manner was important for this book. To borrow from the eminent sociologist Howard Becker, we sought to write in a more accessible and a less obscure, "ceremonial" way (see Becker's 2007 chapter "Persona and Authority"). Becker (2007, 34) says that the desire to be seen as elegant, smart and classy frequently compels social scientists to adopt a writing persona that involves the use of "fancy language, big words for little ones, and elaborate sentences."

With the advent of postmodern and poststructuralist critical theories and their considerable popularity in many disciplines, there has been ongoing critique about the limitations of these perspectives, including their lack of practicality (for example, Leavitt 1999 in the context of Criminology; Woolgar and Pawluch 1985 on social problems theorizing; Sokal, 2008 in the natural sciences; and Norris 1990 and 1992 in literary studies). These critiques are levelled most frequently at "sceptical" postmodernists, who have been described as "pessimistic, negative, [and] gloomy" (Rosenau 1992, 15). Some critics find it easy to discount sceptical postmodernists, viewing them as cynical, even hypercritical, and long on critique but short on constructive solutions. Other critiques of postmodernist and poststructuralist writings are associated with the virtually impenetrable, abstruse writing styles that characterize some postmodern projects. Working through postmodern writings can be gratifying, but this book is not meant to be overly laborious.

Still, theory remains a significant part of this work. As Pfohl (1985, 9) notes, "Theoretical perspectives provide us with an image of what something is and how we might act toward it." This book is an attempt to balance practicality with useful theoretical insights. A single book will not dramatically change the homophobic and transphobic elements of educational institutions, but a book that is both informed by theory and accessible to various people (e.g., educators, students, administrators, politicians, activists, researchers) will hopefully have more impact than one that is limited to abstract theorizing. We tried to make this book stronger by clarifying abstract concepts and terminology and writing for those interested readers who do not have a background in criminological and queer theories.

Aside from language, other challenges we experienced in conducting our research centred around the lack of data from a Canadian context on which to base our study. There have been recent efforts to examine homophobia in a Canadian context. In some instances, however, the threat of a tarnished identity prevents students from reporting harassment, compels school staff to avoid discussing homophobia and transphobia with their peers and students, and dissuades researchers from exploring harassment motivated by the phobias.

We also want to acknowledge two key frameworks that are not developed in this book. First, we did not engage in a thorough analysis of how cultural background, ethnicity, social class, immigration status and other identities that intersect with sexual orientation may have shaped our participants' experiences with HTP. We acknowledge, though, that "oppression cannot be reduced to one fundamental type and that all oppressions work together in producing injustice" (Collins 2000, 18). For example, harassment based on sexual orientation and gender identity may be compounded by racialized discrimination and this may especially be the case for people who identify as two-spirit.

According to Lerat (2004, 6) the term "two-spirit" was originally "used by North American Aboriginal societies to describe what Europeans now call Gay, Lesbian, Bisexual, Transgendered and Transsexual people." Two-spirit was useful for representing male-bodied Aboriginal people who had female intuitions and women who had the physical characteristics of males but still possessed female intuition. Those identified as two-spirit frequently held special status in their communities as spiritual advisors and mediators (Lerat 2004, 6).

Despite holding such coveted statuses in traditional Aboriginal societies, colonization has resulted in the denigration of two-spirit people. The now-defunct Residential School programs in Canada continue to affect two-spirit and other Aboriginal people. Lerat (2004, 6) claims that, "as a direct result of the residential school experience, homophobia is now rampant in most Aboriginal communities, even more so than in mainstream society." Consequently, two-spirit people are often marginalized in mainstream and Aboriginal communities due to their multiple stigmatized identities.

The second area of analysis not explored in this book is cyber-bullying, a phenomenon that is increasing apace with the recent advances in communications technology. Harassment can happen through texting with cellular phones and through almost any social networking site on the Internet. In their 2008 study, the Gay, Lesbian, and Straight Education Network (GLSEN) found that over half of the students in their sample experienced some form of cyber-bullying in the year leading up to the survey (Kosciw, Diaz and Greytak, 2008). In Canada, several organizations and websites have been created to address cyber-bullying and promote safe use of the Internet (e.g., cyberbullying.ca, safecanada.ca, and PREVNet).

One area given extra attention in this book is our intention to leaven the negative, even lethal impact of HTP bullying with some degree of positivity. Optimism about our ability to bring about change in society (a characteristic of "affirmative postmodernism") is an important part of this project (Rosenau 1992, 15). Where oppressive experiences are relayed, we've tried to give voice to the agency and techniques of resistance engaged in by participants as individuals, and possibly as part of an emerging social movement against the oppression of high-school students. Additionally, young people's experiences with supportive teachers or students and the positive effects of their experiences with homophobia and transphobia are presented, accounts often missing from all but the most recent research on HTP in schools. Before presenting findings from our discussions with queer youth in B.C., we turn to some key background information on what is known about homophobic and transphobic bullying.

Chapter 1

Homophobia and Transphobia in Schools

The rights of lesbians, gay men, bisexuals and queer people have been increasingly recognized in Canada in the past two decades. The same cannot be said, however, for trans- people at this point. Beginning in the 1980s, provinces in Canada began to include, or read, sexual orientation into their Human Rights Codes. In 1998, upholding an appeal in the *Vriend v. Alberta* case, Justice Lamer of the Supreme Court of Canada ruled that sexual orientation must be read into an Act protecting individuals against discrimination in Alberta. This decision led other jurisdictions to add sexual orientation as a protected category in human rights legislation. In 2005, Canada became the fourth country to legalize same-sex marriage. Given that same-sex marriage is currently legal in only seven countries worldwide and is outlawed in all but six states within the U.S., the move to legalize same-sex marriage in Canada has been heralded as a victory for the queer community. Despite this progressive legislation, many queer youth are still unable to safely hold hands with their partners in or around their high schools. Legalization of same-sex marriage may have granted symbolic legitimacy to same-sex relationships, but it provides little protection for many queer youth who enter into them.

Whether queer people, and especially queer youth, have benefited from legislative protections in their day-to-day lives seems not to be considered in discussions around human rights laws. Many of us seem to take the legalisation of same-sex marriage, for example, as a sign of how queer people are well-treated in our society. In a Criminology exam invigilated by Rebecca, students were asked whether they believed that queer people in Canada are oppressed. Every student who argued that queer people are not oppressed in Canada (about eight of thirty-seven) made reference to the legalization of same-sex marriage. That such an equation is made is problematic since marriage is but one small segment of life and one that not every queer person desires to be a part of or is eligible for. Many queer people are against same-sex marriage, seeing it as a co-optation into heterosexual culture rather than an acceptance of other sexualities (Park 2007; Rule 2001). On this note, Leung (2008, 100) argues:

> Following the recent legalization of gay marriage in the Netherlands, Belgium, Spain, and Canada, the marriage issue has received intense global attention. The debates have been predominantly framed as

either-or positions, assuming an automatic equation between queer interests and support for gay marriage. What is often missing in mainstream debates is the complex discussion within queer communities, where objections to marriage are rooted in a critique of its normalizing effect and of its nonrecognition of sexual practices and affective alliances that fall outside of the parameters of monogamous spousal relations.

Aside from concerns about reinforcing monogamous relationships, same-sex marriage has other limitations. Some queer people are not eligible for marriage, even with its extension to same-sex partners. Youth who identify as lesbian, gay, bisexual or queer may not be immediately affected by changes to marriage laws. Legalization of same-sex marriage might secure future plans to marry and provide an opportunity for debate in classrooms, but participants in this study indicated that class debates about gay marriage took place despite a lack of protection of the rights of queer youth in their schools. Rather than affirming the rights and value of queer people, the debates often resulted in homophobic comments that went unchallenged, at least on the part of school officials. In sum, even in what may be perceived as a liberal climate that has led to an equal footing for everyone regardless of sexual orientation, reactions to homosexuality and gender variance in the day-to-day lives of queer people, and especially queer youth, are often oppressive.

Considering the multicultural climate of Canada, it is also wise to consider how LGBTTQ people are viewed around the world. Canada is home to people of various nationalities and cultures who hold varied beliefs and values. According to Citizenship and Immigration of Canada (2007), a greater number of permanent residents, temporary foreign workers and foreign students entered Canada in 2007 than ever before. Some immigrants travel to Canada from countries where what is seen as same-sex sexual behaviours (usually anal sex) are against the law. Tin's introduction to *The Dictionary of Homophobia* (2008, 11) is quoted at length here to provide an overview of conceptions of homosexuality worldwide:

> Truth be told, the twentieth century was, without a doubt, the most violently homophobic period in history: deportation to concentration camps under the Nazi regime, gulags in the Soviet Union, and blackmail and persecution in the United States during the Joseph McCarthy anti-communist era. For some, particularly in the western world, much of this seems very much part of the past. But quite often living conditions for gays, lesbians, and transgenders in today's world remain very difficult. Homosexuality seems to be discriminated against everywhere: in at least seventy nations, homosexual acts are still illegal (e.g., Algeria, Cameroon, Ethiopia, Kuwait, Lebanon,

and Senegal) and in a good many of these, punishment can last more than ten years (India, Jamaica, Libya, Malaysia, Nigeria, and Syria). Sometimes the law dictates life imprisonment (Guyana and Uganda), and, in a dozen or so nations, the death penalty may be applied (Iran, Mauritania, Saudi Arabia, and Sudan).

In a recent article in *The Georgia Straight*, Bryers (2008) noted that two Iranian citizens were executed in 2007 for homosexuality. Clearly, the conditions Tin speaks of are not merely remnants of unenforced laws that have yet to be repealed.

Given the current climate queer people face throughout the world, we question how anyone could believe that queer people are not oppressed regardless of which national borders surround them. Extraordinary assumptions about the position of queer people in our society cannot be made without exploring the ordinary experiences of our everyday lives. These arguments are even more relevant in regards to the social standing of transgender people in Canada.

Many of us assume that rights and protections awarded to LGBQ people are extended to transgender ("trans") people as well. Some trans people identify with a lesbian, gay, bisexual or queer sexuality and are legally protected from discrimination based on sexual orientation. Nevertheless, gender identity itself is not included in our national human rights legislation. In fact, the Northwest Territories is the only region in Canada with legislation against discrimination based on gender identity. In some cases, other jurisdictions allow complaints under the general "gender" or "sex" category of Human Rights Codes (Luhtanen 2005). In 2009 Bill Siksay, a Member of Parliament in B.C., tabled a Bill for the third time to add gender identity and expression to the Canadian Human Rights Act (Smith 2009). Even so, legislation does not always translate into safety for those whom the laws are designed to protect. The lack of legal protections for trans people coupled with the widespread assumption that GLB rights are extended to transgender individuals may contribute to ongoing harassment of trans people in Canada.

Schools seem like a logical starting place to educate people about the natural occurrence of homosexuality and gender variance in our society. To date, however, school administrators and officials seem to balk at such suggestions. There are various reasons for this. The first and biggest impediment may be the problem-identification process in the educational system. Problem identification is a socially constructed process involving various "claimsmakers" who have a stake in the issue (Howlett and Ramesh 2003) and who compete for attention and resources (Dunn 2004). Gusfield (as cited in Dunn 2004, 459) acknowledges that the recognition of a problem is "not determined by the prevalence, seriousness, or significance of the issue, but by the power and influence of its spokespersons." In the case of HTP bullying in schools, it is clear that those most affected (LGBTTQ youth) may not hold much clout in public or private venues where these debates take place. Consequently, the identification of homophobic and transphobic bullying as an issue worthy of attention has hinged on community activists, parents, government officials and school administrators.

Second, it can be argued that a majority of the stakeholders acting on behalf of students prefer to address bullying in general, rather than to specifically identify and attend to homophobic and transphobic bullying (Walton 2004). Some educators and parents see HTP bullying as inappropriate subject matter in schools because of its association with homosexuality and with sexuality in general (Pascoe 2007). Discussions about homosexuality often evoke strong feelings and the topic becomes exceptionally contentious in the context of schooling, where discussions of sexuality are often stifled and where adults are concerned with children's well-being. As Birden (2005, 2) says:

> Public education… has been placed in the unenviable position of serving the… roles of preserving traditional values while promulgating desirable social evolution.… When issues regarding lesbian and gay people surface in the context of schools, a host of players emerge who attempt to influence school policy by galvanizing public opinion and influencing legislative action. Often, however, sexual diversity issues never get as far as public debate. School-teachers and administrators routinely avoid such conflicts by conflating gay and lesbian identity with "talk about sex" and labelling both "age-inappropriate."

Aside from these two impediments to identifying HTP as a problem in schools, many people automatically assume that high-school students are heterosexual and that their gender identities are fixed. Combined with the assumption that homophobia only affects those who identify with a homosexual orientation, the presumed heterosexuality of students justifies the decision not to address HTP bullying (Youdell 2004). Although these assumptions persist, they have also been challenged. This trend is pronounced in B.C., where queer activists have been increasingly focusing on the education system. In several B.C. Human Rights Tribunal decisions, members of school boards and public servants in the Ministry of Education have been held accountable for providing an educational environment that reflects and respects the diversity of the Canadian population.

Controversies surrounding the inclusion of books depicting same-sex families in classrooms throughout Canada provide examples in which sexual orientation is at the heart of disputes. Although similar reactions occurred when such books were introduced in Calgary, Alberta, and Milton, Ontario, the most notorious case of queer "book banning" centred on an elementary school in Surrey, B.C. (Warner 2002, 339). In 1997, James Chamberlain, an elementary school teacher, requested permission from the Surrey School District 36 to use three books depicting same-sex families to teach his kindergarten and Grade 1 students about diversity. Under pressure from parents and various conservative and religious groups, school board members refused this request, instigating a lengthy human rights complaint that culminated at the Supreme Court of Canada. In finding the "Board's decision not to approve the proposed books depicting same-sex parented families ... unreasonable" (*Chamberlain v. Surrey School District No. 36* 2002, preamble, para. 9), the Right Honourable Beverly McLachlin stated:

> Exposure to some cognitive dissonance is arguably necessary if children are to be taught what tolerance itself involves.... The demand for tolerance cannot be interpreted as the demand to approve of another person's beliefs or practices. When we ask people to be tolerant of others, we do not ask them to abandon their personal convictions. We merely ask them to respect the rights, values and ways of being of those who may not share those convictions.... Learning about tolerance is therefore learning that other people's entitlement to respect from us does not depend on whether their views accord with our own. Children cannot learn this unless they are exposed to views that differ from those they are taught at home. (*Chamberlain v. Surrey School District No. 36* 2002, para. 66)

In the ruling, in which two judges dissented, the judges directed the members of the school board to reconsider their decision to ban the books, taking into consideration the guiding principles of "tolerance and non-sectarianism underlying the School Act, R.S.B.C. 1996, c. 412" (*Pegura et al. v. School District No. 36* 2003, para. 3). That the School Act was referred to, and not the Charter of Freedom and Rights, is remarkable. A reference to the Charter would likely have had more persuasive power than suggesting that school board trustees consider guiding principles of tolerance.

Also in B.C., in 1999, Peter and Murray Corren, then Peter Cook and Murray Warren, filed a complaint with the British Columbia Human Rights Tribunal (BCHRT). In the complaint they accused the Ministry of Education of systemic discrimination against "non-heterosexual students and their parents" for excluding same-sex parents, sexual orientation and gender identity from the curriculum (*Cook and Warren v. Ministry of Education* 2003, para. 2). The Correns argued that the silence surrounding same-sex relationships in the curriculum bred an atmosphere of ignorance and intolerance towards sexual minorities ("School System Accused" 2005) and that schools were ill-equipped to deal with the homophobic and transphobic bullying that results from such oversights (*Corren and Corren v. B.C.* 2005, para. 35).

Before the 2006 trial began, the Correns reached an agreement — referred to as "the Corren agreement" — with the provincial government whereby authorities agreed to review the current curriculum for inclusiveness. The agreement also gave the couple an "unprecedented right to have direct input into the content of the whole of the British Columbia school curriculum so as to make it more inclusive of and responsive to the queer community and its history and culture" (Murray and Peter Corren Foundation n.d., n.p.). Following up on the agreement, in June 2006 the B.C. Attorney General announced an elective course for Grade 12 students focusing on social justice issues, including sexual orientation. Three years later, controversy about "Social Justice 12" persisted, as at least one district opted not to offer the course in their schools. In response, students in Abbotsford held several protests, culminating in a march that attracted hundreds of people from the Lower Mainland who rallied to support the queer youth. Since then, the Abbotsford School Board announced that it would run the Social Justice course in the fall of 2009 ("Abbotsford School Board Permits" 2009).

Concerns about homophobic bullying came to the fore in 2003 when Azmi Jubran placed a complaint with the Human Rights Commission in British Columbia. Jubran was subjected to constant taunting and bullying behaviours throughout his time in a North Vancouver high school. In a decision that eventually went to the Supreme Court of B.C., Judges found that Jubran was discriminated against on the basis of his perceived sexual orientation. In his 2005 ruling, Justice Stewart stated that the homophobic harassment was harmful and violated the Charter because it was directed at someone *perceived* to be gay (Jubran did not identify as gay) (Board of School Trustees 2003). Justice Stewart found that Jubran's dignity and full participation in school were denied, and he placed blame on the North Vancouver School Board for the discrimination through their failure to provide a harassment-free environment.

This case sent a strong message to educational administrators that merely reprimanding students for discriminatory actions was inadequate. Justice Stewart demanded that the school board provide a clear statement of conduct regarding homophobic bullying and ensure that it is communicated to all students. He also ruled that school staff should be provided with appropriate training and resources to prevent discrimination and harassment from occurring (Continuing Legal Education Society of British Columbia 2005). Jubran was awarded $4,500 in damages and the school board was ordered to cover his legal costs (GALE BC n.d.).

Human rights cases involving queer youth have been instigated in other parts of Canada as well. In Ontario, despite collecting over six hundred signatures from people supporting his initiatives to raise awareness about homophobia in his Sault Ste. Marie high school, student Jeremy Dias felt he continually met with resistance on the part of his administrators. In 2002, after graduating from the school, Dias filed a human rights complaint against the Algoma District School Board. He asked only that members of the school board apologize and allow one gay-friendly poster to be placed in the halls of his former high school. The school board refused and settled out of court in 2005. Dias used the undisclosed amount of settlement money to establish Jer's Vision: Canada's Youth Diversity Initiative, which provides scholarships for LGBTTQ youth (Moran 2005).

In 2002, Marc Hall, a Grade 12 student in Oshawa, Ontario, brought his principal and the Durham Catholic District School Board to court for refusing to let him bring his boyfriend to the school prom (see Callaghan 2007 for more on homophobia in Canadian Catholic schools). The principal, who was later supported by the school board, stated that "interacting with a same sex partner at the prom would constitute a form of sexual activity that contravened the teachings of the Catholic Church" (Grace and Wells 2005, 8). Noting the competing interests in the case, Justice MacKinnon stated:

> It is one of the distinguishing strengths of Canada as a nation that we value tolerance and respect for others. All of us have fundamental rights including expression, association and religion. Sometimes, as in this case, our individual rights bump into those of our neighbours and of our institutions. When that occurs we, as individuals and as institutions, must acknowledge the duties that accompany our rights. Mr. Hall has a duty to accord to others who do not share his orientation the respect that they, with their religious values and beliefs, are due. Conversely, for the reasons I have given, the Principal and the Board have a duty to accord to Mr. Hall the respect that he is due as he attends the Prom with his date, his classmates and their dates. (*Hall (Litigation guardian of) v. Powers* 2002, para. 60)

Although the lawsuit was not resolved before the prom night, Marc Hall was granted an injunction allowing him and his boyfriend to attend his school prom just hours before it commenced. Three years later, Hall dropped the case before it was adjudicated.

These court and tribunal decisions illustrate a growing concern on behalf of LGBTTQ advocates and judiciaries to promote inclusiveness and safety for queer people in schools. They also illustrate the increasing recognition of the duty of school officials to address homophobic and transphobic harassment in schools. Legal and financial costs provide school administrators with an impetus to at least appear as though they are taking action, even if many of their constituents disagree with anti-homophobia/transphobia efforts.

Recently, there have been several initiatives in Canadian educational systems to provide a safer milieu for queer youth.

In 2003, the British Columbia Safe School Task Force released a report regarding bullying, harassment and intimidation in schools. Bullying based on one's sexual orientation (or perceived sexual orientation) was recognized as a significant problem in British Columbia schools. The Task Force urged school board officials to adopt policies and programs consistent with "values and categories" detailed in the B.C. Human Rights Code and the Charter of Rights and Freedoms (Gilbert 2004; Mayencourt, Locke and McMahon 2003).

Sexual orientation and gender identity do not explicitly appear in the Charter of Rights and Freedoms. Nevertheless, in the 1995 case of *Egan and Nesbit v. Canada*, a judge decided that sexual orientation was an "analogous ground to other characteristics of persons" covered in s. 15 (Grace 2005, n.p.). In other words, sexual orientation, and, arguably, gender identity should be read into the existing legislation. In addition, the B.C. Human Rights Code specifically outlines the rights to protections against discrimination that should be afforded to lesbians, gay men and bisexual people (Human Rights Code 1996). Since the Task Force report, school boards in Southeast Kootenay, Victoria, Vancouver, the Gulf Islands, North Vancouver, Prince Rupert and Revelstoke have adopted policies that prohibit discrimination on the basis of sexual orientation or gender identity (GALE BC n.d.), and other districts continue to advocate for policies (Steffenhagen 2009).

Teaching federations in Alberta and British Columbia have also adopted policies that prohibit discrimination based on sexual orientation. In 2003 the Alberta Teachers' Association (ATA) became the first teachers' association in Canada "to include gender identity as a prohibited ground for discrimination" (Schrader and Wells 2005, 4). Recently, however, these efforts have been threatened by a proposed law (Bill 44) that would "enshrine the words 'sexual orientation' in the province's Human Rights Act" but also enable parents to keep their children from participating in "lessons that involve religion, sexual orientation and sexuality" (Hasselriis 2009, para. 3).

Homophobia and transphobia are gradually being recognized in other parts of Canada. For example, in 1994, the Toronto District School Board (TDSB) introduced the Triangle Program, the first alternative secondary school in Canada for LGBTTQ youth affected by homophobia. In the program, queer youth, many of whom were close to dropping (or being forced) out of mainstream high schools, earn their high school diploma. The realities of LGBTTQ students are reflected in the curriculum that "includes and celebrates LGBT literature, history, persons, and issues" (Triangle Program n.d.). There is debate about whether a dedicated school program for queer youth is the best option. In response to this debate, and the increased awareness about homophobia in schools, the TDSB introduced the Human Sexuality Program, designed to provide support to LGBTTQ students within the mainstream school system (Dwyer and Farran 1997). We were unable to find out whether this program had any impact on levels of homophobic and transphobic harassment in Toronto-area schools.

Prevalence of Homophobic Bullying

While researchers have written about homosexuality for more than fifty years, academics have only increasingly focused on the lives of queer youth in the past two decades. Savin-Williams (1990, 9) ties the earliest research on gay youth to a study conducted in 1972 by Roesler and Deisher. The study was designed to "assist physicians and counsellors who might want to intervene in the lives of prehomosexual boys." Indeed, much of the early research on queer individuals was the product of medical fields focusing on the homosexual (and male) body itself. More recently, however, health and social science researchers in Canada have been exploring how others' opinions and beliefs about homosexuality can affect the queer individual.

In 2008, advocates with Egale Canada, along with Dr. Catherine Taylor at the University of Winnipeg, launched the first National Climate Survey on homophobia in Canadian high schools (see www.climatesurvey.ca for details). This ongoing study is designed to measure how supportive Canadian students feel their schools are of homosexuality. The study met with controversy in some areas, with school board officials declining to participate or even promote the survey in their jurisdictions ("Catholic Schools Reject" 2008). At best, these refusals underscore continuing anxieties about discussing homosexuality and transgenderism in schools; at worst, they speak to the enduring presence of homophobia and transphobia within educational institutions.

With a total sample of twelve hundred youth thus far, results from the first phase of the Egale study show that 73 percent of LGBTQ students felt unsafe in at least one place in school compared to 49 percent of heterosexual students. (Egale Canada 2009). Sixty percent of queer youth in that sample reported having been verbally harassed and 25 percent reported experiencing physical harassment because of their sexual orientation. In regards to cyberbullying, over 31 percent of students had hurtful rumours spread about them by electronic means (Egale Canada 2009).

In addition to this nationwide study, some quantitative data have been generated in B.C. Researchers at the University of British Columbia published results from a research study exploring experiences of lesbian, gay, bisexual and questioning (or unsure) youth in eighteen B.C. high schools. This sample of lesbian and gay youth reported levels of verbal, physical and social harassment that were up to 80 percent higher than their heterosexual peers (Darwich

2008). The McCreary Centre Society in B.C. has published several studies on queer, high-school-aged youth. In their recent B.C. Adolescent Health Survey, researchers found that over 60 percent of high-school-aged youth who identified as gay or lesbian and about 50 percent of bisexuals reported verbal harassment from their peers (Saewyc et al. 2007). Similarly, in his pioneering thesis about anti-lesbian/gay violence in the Greater Vancouver area, Samis (1995, 80) found that 61 percent of 327 queer respondents said they had experienced homophobic slurs while at school.

Queer youth may also be socially excluded or isolated from their heterosexual peers. Youth in the McCreary Centre sample were almost twice as likely as heterosexual youth to report deliberate exclusion (54 percent of gay and lesbian youth and 46 percent bisexual vs. 30 percent heterosexual) (Saewyc et al. 2007). Students may feel isolated as a result of hurtful homophobic slurs. Cochrane and Morrison (2008) found that 52 percent of the fifty-four high-school-aged youth in their Saskatchewan sample reported frequently hearing words such as "fag," "dyke," "homo" or "lezzie" in their schools. In Ontario-based studies of young gay men (Smith 1998) and lesbians (Khayatt 1994), participants reported that homophobic speech was a common occurrence in their high schools. In fact, the PFLAG Canada website indicates that some LGBT students hear "anti-gay" insults about twenty-six times a day (PFLAG Canada 2009). In addition, George Smith (1998, 320) reported that the gay male youth he spoke to in Ontario frequently encountered homophobic graffiti such as "kill the faggot." In the U.S., researchers with the Gay, Lesbian, and Straight Education Network (GLSEN) produce reports documenting the school experiences of students from kindergarten to Grade 12. In their 2009 study, they determined that nine out of ten youth reported hearing "gay" used in a negative context, and the majority of these students said that they were bothered by such use (Kosciw, Diaz and Greytak 2008).

George Smith (1998, 320) asserts that the "logical conclusion" of subtle forms of anti-gay abuse is physical violence. Research indicates that physical forms of homophobic harassment persist. Compared to their heterosexual counterparts, twice as many bisexual males (13 percent vs. 28 percent) and four times as many bisexual females and lesbians (5 percent vs. 20 percent and 19 percent respectively) in the latest McCreary Centre sample said that peers at school had physically assaulted them in the year before the survey (Saewyc et al. 2007). Also in Canada, Samis (1995) found that approximately 20 percent of the lesbians and gay men in his sample were physically attacked at school (22.4 percent of 303 respondents). Unfortunately, these Canadian studies fail to include any exact definition of physical harassment, an oversight that has been addressed by some academics in the U.S.

Perhaps because of Canada's reputation for tolerance, or simply because of a lack of research in the area here, studies conducted in the U.S. indicate that high-school bullying motivated by gender or sexual identity is more prevalent than levels reported by Canadian researchers (see, for example, Douglas et al. 1999; Stepp 2001). In their nationwide U.S. study for the Gay, Lesbian, and Straight Education Network (GLSEN; Kosciw, Diaz and Greytak 2008, 20) found that about 44 percent of the youth in their sample were assaulted (pushed or shoved) due to their sexual orientation, and 22 percent were punched, kicked or injured with a weapon. It is no wonder that more than 60 percent of the youth in their sample felt unsafe at school because of their sexual orientation (Kosciw, Diaz and Greytak, 2008, 25).

Heterosexual students are also subject to harassment motivated by gender or sexual identity in schools. In the 1993 Adolescent Health Survey, researchers at the McCreary Centre in B.C. found that 4 percent of male students and 3 percent of female students believed they were discriminated against or harassed based on their perceived sexual orientation (as cited in Gilbert 2004). Often these heterosexual youth fail to conform to "hegemonic [or dominant] understandings of masculinity and femininity" (Valentine, Butler and Skelton 2001, 121; see also Blumenfeld 1992; Pascoe 2007).

Gramsci (1971, 12) conceived hegemony as "spontaneous consent given by the great masses of the population to the general direction imposed on social life by the dominant fundamental group." Hegemony helps explain why subordinate groups go along with and even participate in practices that are not in their own best interest and may even be detrimental to them (Artz and Murphy 2000). Hegemonic masculinity is useful, for example, in our understanding that men are not a monolithic grouping; instead, some men enjoy greater status and privilege than others. Hegemonic masculinity is seen as an ideal of maleness that might include being able-bodied, athletic, white, heterosexual, among other attributes. According to Raewyn Connell's formulation of hegemonic masculinity, men who do not measure up to a particular hegemonic idea may be "subordinated" or "marginalized" in this hierarchy of maleness, and this could include, for instance, gay men and transgender men (see Levy 2007, 253–54).

Despite growing attention to homophobia in schools, there has been little done to learn more about transphobia. In her work on "gendered harassment," Meyer (2008, 8) discusses how stereotypes equating homosexuality with gender inversion cause people who fail to conform to traditional gender norms (including trans people) to be labelled gay or lesbian and to experience homophobia. Still, there has been little emphasis on gender, and specifically transgenders, in discourse surrounding bullying.

Prevalence of Transphobic Bullying

> The threat of violence toward transgendered persons, particularly transgendered youth who must attend community schools, is made all the more powerful by the fact that they do not have to do anything to receive the violence. It is their lives alone that precipitate such action. Therefore, transpersons always have a sense of safety which is fragile and tenuous and they may never feel completely secure. (Mallon 2000, 11)

Despite indications that many children or adolescents feel at odds with their sex and assigned gender (Gagné, Tewksbury and McGaughey 1997), most do not adopt a transgender or transsexual identity until their twenties or even thirties. Children learn early on that violating gender norms can result in stigmatization, hostility and isolation (Gagné and Tewksbury 1998). The socialization process is difficult to undo and many trans people suppress their "authentic selves" for as long as possible (Gagné and Tewksbury 1998, 87). This suppression may be one reason why there is so little information on the experiences of trans youth in schools.

Much of what we know about trans youth is limited to clinical fields, where trans people are portrayed as pathological and in need of treatment, or to fields that focus on sex reassignment (Burgess 1999; Leung 2008; Wyss 2004). Researchers with Human Rights Watch (Bochenek and Widney 2001, in their section "Transgender Youth") point out that, "if gay and lesbian people have achieved some modicum of acceptance in the United States over the past several decades, transgender people remain misunderstood at best and vilified at worst."

Burgess (1999, 35) concludes that trans youth are "among the most neglected, misunderstood groups in our society today." Adolescence may be an especially challenging time for trans people because changes associated with puberty, which often coincide with greater demands for gender conformity, can heighten feelings of confusion and isolation. Sometimes trans youth feel repelled by or ashamed of developing sexual characteristics, which can even lead to extreme attempts to remove unwanted sex organs (cutting or beating oneself) and hormone or steroid abuse (Burgess 1999, 43).

Youth who identify as transgender and who wish to transition to the "other" gender may be more vulnerable to discipline of their bodies due to their limited resources and the cost of surgery (Gender Public Advocacy Coalition 2006). Those who do decide to go through the transition process are subject to a waiting period of from one to two years (Shelley 2008). In the interim, trans youth often present an identity that is less likely to "pass," and they are more likely to experience harassment. In addition, many aspects of high school emphasize gender differences (e.g., gender-segregated gym classes, school dances) and highlight differences between trans youth and gender-conforming peers (Burgess 1999). Mallon (1999, 58) puts it bluntly: "Schools... are among the least affirming environments of all for gender-variant children."

We were unable to find any Canadian human rights cases involving youth who identify as transgender, or research focusing specifically on the "T" in the LGBT youth population. However, in the first national study on homophobia in schools in Canada, Egale Canada (2009) focused some questions on the experiences of trans youth. The preliminary findings from this research indicate that 87 percent of trans youth feel unsafe in at least one place in their school. These feelings were likely justified, as 82 percent of the trans students in the sample reported they had been verbally harassed and 39 percent had been physically harassed because of their gender. In addition, 33 percent of trans students had heard negative comments about not being "manly" enough and 35 percent, comments about not being "feminine" enough (Egale Canada 2009). While this research is groundbreaking, we still know very little about the experiences of trans youth and the impact of HTP on them.

In interviews with twenty transgender adults in the Greater Vancouver district of B.C., Shelley (2008) asked about their experiences in educational settings. Some reported dropping out of high school, due in part to the bullying they endured. Jamie-Lee said:

> I was teased because I was a very slight, effeminate boy. You know, there was the name calling and that kind of stuff.... I dropped out in grade ten [and it was]... definitely due to the gender issues. (Shelley 2008, 88)

Those who stayed in high school reported verbal and physical abuse. Although the interviews were not designed to determine the frequency of transphobia in high schools on a large scale, Shelley's exploratory study helps to illustrate what some trans people experienced.

Most information about discrimination and violence against trans people in North America has come from the U.S. Researchers at the Gay, Lesbian, and Straight Education Network (GLSEN) focused more on gender identity in recent School Climate Surveys than in the past. In their report on safety in high school, the authors found that trans youth "reported higher levels of victimization than all other students" (Kosciw et al. 2008, 59). Two-thirds of youth in their sample reported verbal harassment in school related to their gender expression (Kosciw et al. 2008, 30). Negative comments were made by both students and teachers and were most often directed at males who were not "masculine enough" (Kosciw et al. 2008). Almost one-third (30.4 percent) of youth were pushed or shoved and 14 percent were physically assaulted outright (i.e., punched, kicked, or injured with a weapon) due to their gender expression. In all, 38 percent of the youth in this sample reported feeling unsafe at school because of their gender expression.

Other research in the U.S. seems to confirm that trans youth are not only victimized more often, but may experience more severe forms of victimization. In New York, researchers interviewed and surveyed eight trans youth. These youth were frequently harassed by both classmates and teachers, who were attempting to enforce what they saw as gender-appropriate behaviour. The young people were told to "stop acting like a girl" and were even called faggots and sissies by their own teachers (Bochenek and Widney 2001). In another study, Wyss (2004, 716–17) found that twenty-three of their twenty-four young trans and genderqueer participants from throughout the U.S. experienced some degree of victimization in high school, eleven of whom experienced physical violence or sexual assaults. These experiences ranged from being pushed, shoved and smacked to being raped or set on fire (Wyss 2004). A research team from Philadelphia reported that 83 percent of the twenty-four trans youth they spoke with had experienced "physical abuse and torment" at school, including "being followed, pushed, shoved, punched, and beaten; having objects thrown at them, and in some cases, being assaulted with weapons" (Sausa 2005, 19).

From what we have learned about violence against trans people in general, harassment meted out in schools continues later on in life. Researchers with the Gender Public Advocacy Coalition (GenderPAC) published two important studies about experiences of trans people in the U.S. In the first study, Lombardi, Wilchins, Priesling and Malouf (2001, 95) found that nearly 60 percent of the 402 trans people (of any age) in their nationwide sample reported some form of harassment or violence based on their gender expression and 47 percent had been physically assaulted. Most important for our purposes, the researchers found that younger people in their sample were more likely to experience violence than older people and are often "scorned, attacked and locked or thrown out of their homes" (Lombardi et al. 2001, 98).

In 2006, the GenderPAC released a report called "50 Under 30" documenting the murders of fifty trans people under the age of thirty from 1995 to 2005. The authors concluded that if gender identity were included as a hate crime in the U.S., murders based on gender nonconformity would be second only to hate crimes based on race (Gender Public Advocacy Coalition 2006, 2). The researchers estimate that on average five trans youth were murdered in the U.S. per year from 1995 to 2005 (a total of fifty). Sixteen of the victims were teenagers; the youngest victim was only fifteen years old. Biological males, youth of colour, and poor youth were most likely to be victimized (Gender Public Advocacy Coalition 2006).

Trans activist and scholar Susan Stryker has drawn attention to the overrepresentation of male-to-female trans victims in crime statistics. At a conference in 1999, she argued that 2 percent of the violence reported by trans people is aimed at trans men (female to male) while an astonishing 98 percent is reported by trans women (male to female) (as cited in Denike, Renshaw and Rowe 2003). It should be noted, however, that researchers in the United Kingdom found that trans men (female to male) in their sample were more likely to report having experienced transphobic harassment while in high school than trans women (male to female) (Whittle, Turner and Al-Alami 2007). The gender of the attacker is also important: all known perpetrators in the second GenderPAC study were males who attacked biological males close to their own age (Gender Public Advocacy Coalition 2006, 5). In general, as previous research shows, and as this book will illustrate, it is important to acknowledge gender nonconformity as a distinct basis of harassment, but also to note the gender of those involved when examining and addressing transphobic bullying.

In sum, there is evidence that gender-nonconforming youth may experience harassment at higher rates than some of their queer counterparts (Bochenek and Widney 2001; Messerschmidt 2007; Varjas et al. 2007). Yet, there is little research documenting the effects of HTP on trans youth specifically and even less about positive experiences of these young people in school. Although none of the youth we spoke with identified as trans, some identified as "genderqueer" or used other terms to express the fluid nature of their gender, which they felt could not be identified within the traditional masculine or feminine frameworks. Almost all of our participants, though, relayed experiences where they were bullied because of their gender expressions.

Chapter 2

Experiences of HTP in High School

As mentioned in Chapter One, bullying in schools has truly become a "hot topic" in the mass media and in academia. Representations of bullying by journalists and academics, however, do not always reflect students' everyday experiences. In their attempt to provide sensational accounts of the events they cover, media representatives rarely address underlying motives for bullying behaviours. In addition, media outlets, academics, schools administrators and educators focus on more obvious, physical forms of harassment even though, as Meyer (2006, 43) argues, "verbal harassment is more prevalent and... equally damaging to students," and certainly there is more awareness of online bullying such as postings on Facebook and other websites (Li 2006; Shariff 2008; Szklarski 2008).

Walton (2006, 17) likens discourse around bullying, including media reports, to the "society of the spectacle" in which sensational and violent incidents appear normative. While this may be true of the discourse, it is not the case for the bullying behaviours themselves. For study participants, physical violence was one of the least frequent forms of homophobic or transphobic harassment they encountered. Homophobic or transphobic name-calling, avoidance, exclusion, and heterosexist or gender-limiting environments were more common than physical forms of harassment.

Physical Harassment

> Snow days were the worst though, because I'd have to walk home, and on a snow day, everyone decides to throw snowballs, and, oh, choose the one wearing the pink t-shirt!... "Get that freak!" (Nadeem, gay, male)

Accounts of homophobic bullying often include moving narratives by sexual minorities who were physically brutalized in or near schools (O'Connor 1995; Olweus 1993). Such brutal experiences do not square with reports from most of our participants. Still, three of the sixteen participants had been assaulted, and four (two of whom had experienced violence themselves) had witnessed other students being physically assaulted because of their sexual orientation or gender identity. The number of young people who reported experiencing physical violence in our study (about one-quarter) is in line with the other research (Egale Canada 2009; Kosciw and Diaz 2006; Samis 1995; Saewyc et al. 2007). Physical harassment ranged from being pelted with snowballs (a story Nadeem shared in the opening quotation) to being beaten unconscious. At least three participants feared physical reprisals if they were perceived as queer. One expressed fear of other males in high school:

> It was easier for me to be around girls. I guess I could be a little more... gay or whatever... and there was less of that fear of, I don't know, punishment or something because, right, it's sexist, but a guy would be able to injure me more than a girl, right? (Jamie, queer/gay, *)

Generally speaking, the queer youth experienced physical violence mostly from young men and in certain contexts where teachers were not often present or where physical aggressiveness was accepted.

Physical Harassment: Context
Physical Education (P.E.) classes are one locus of HTP bullying (Smith 1998). In this sense, "physical education" takes on a new meaning as physical forms of violence teach students about the importance of mainstream gender norms. Interviewees were also shoved around in change rooms before or after P.E. classes as well as on off-school property. These are environments where there are usually no teachers to intervene and where being roughed up can be passed off as legitimate. Discussing P.E. classes, participants relayed their experiences with violence:

> A couple of friends of mine had to be removed from PE for their safety.... At the time PE was compulsory up until Grade 10.... There were a couple of guys who I guess were especially flamey. Like my friend... he was just... on fire. And he and this other guy... the boys' P.E. class just attacked them. (Sam, queer/gay, queer)

> There was a kid that I knew in a younger grade.... I was in math class, and he was in gym class, and he came and talked to me, because he said that they were playing Ultimate [Frisbee], like a Frisbee game, outside on the field and that they were purposely throwing the Frisbee over his head to tackle him and beat him up. (Heather, *, female)

Sykes (2004) and Messerschmidt (2000) note the tendency for people to associate athleticism with masculine heterosexuality. The "jock" culture was associated with homophobic and transphobic behaviour by at least two people in this study. Speaking about a classmate who often taunted him, calling him "faggot," Trevor said:

> It was kind of okay because he wasn't like a hardcore jock or anything. Even the jocks didn't really like him... so I was just kind of like, whatever, I don't care about you. (gay, male)

Phoenix believed that males, and especially "jocks," were responsible for most of the physical aggression:

> With physical or aggressive situations it was always males. And it always seemed like the kind of guys who had something to prove. Either they were tough guys or bullies or jocks... they weren't really the quiet academic-y type of guys, they were always kind of the more aggressive sorts to begin with. But they were always male, in my experience. (queer, androgynous)

Here Phoenix refers to gender, a theme that surfaced throughout the focus groups and interviews. All but one of the former students who were targeted physically were male and almost all of the aggressors were male. Other researchers have made similar assertions about the gender of the target and physical harasser in their studies on HTP (Meyer 2006; Nayak and Kehily 1996; Pascoe 2007; Smith 1998). The only exception to both trends in our study came from Haley (lesbian/queer, female) who spoke of her experience with physical HTP harassment:

> Haley: Guys, girls, everything, it was all vicious. If it was coming at us, it was vicious.
> RH: And it was guys and girls?
> Haley: Oh yeah...
> RH: And, would the girls be violent as well, or...
> Haley: Oh yeah. Yep!

Some of the girls who Haley said engaged in physical harassment were part of the jock culture. Haley described girls with whom she had run-ins:

> Usually, if it was girls, it wasn't preppy girls. It was either pucks... [RH: The what?] The pucks. The... hockey... teams... girls. They go around everyone on the team! Or the girls that just happened to be overweight and insecure... it was never just the regular girls. They were always fine.

According to her, even "straight" students were not spared from the jocks' homophobic and transphobic physical abuse.

My friend... and his girlfriend were going together for a long time.... The hockey guys [attacked] him from behind... called him gay, called him a fag... and they said, "If you want it that way, we'll give it that way," and started beating on him.

Linking athleticism and heterosexuality meant that unathletic males and females who excelled at contact sports were frequently typecast as gay or lesbian. Asked who was most likely to experience HTP harassment, Sam said, "Boys, effeminate boys especially [were] targeted a lot, especially in gym class..." (queer/gay, queer). Although young men and women experience harassment related to gender variance, participants thought that males in their high schools were most likely to be harassed for not meeting the expectation of hegemonic masculinity. As Walton (2006) notes, though, it may be that females experience more subtle forms of HTP harassment that are less noticeable and often not acknowledged.

In short, some queer youth — especially males — dread P.E. class and changing for the class because they find themselves easy targets of insults and physical harassment. Speaking of harassment that took place in change rooms, participants said:

In the change rooms... I'd get a lot of, like, "What the fuck are you looking at? Faggot!" that kind of stuff. And I had a couple of people try to throw me into the locker, but I fought [back]. (Trystan, gay, male)

It was mostly in gym class, and the locker room was kind of awkward. (Trevor, gay, male)

When I was on the football team, it gets kind of awkward in the football change room. (Demetrius, gay, male)

Following these comments, others added:

Lukas: That's usually why I changed in the bathroom. (bisexual, male)
Xander: Me too! I was just using the one stall that we had. Every time, that's where I was. (gay/homosexual, male)
Trevor: Yep, me too. (gay, male)
Lukas: It was just easier to just not have to deal with it.

Change rooms were places where many queer students felt unsafe, or at least uncomfortable, sites where bodies were bared, unprotected and open to scrutiny. Gender-segregated spaces increase demands for adherence to gender norms and require one to prove that they belong there. Lavatories, another gender-segregated environment, can be distressing for people who do not easily fit the either male or female gender categories associated with these spaces (Pazos 1999; Sausa 2005; Scholinski 1997; Shelley 2008). Sam referred to the importance of gender norms in change rooms:

> I avoided joining the basketball team in high school even though I likely would have made the team because many of the "popular" girls tried out for the team and I wanted to avoid the highly gendered environment of a change room policed by the "popular" girls. (queer/gay, queer)

Persistent, negative stereotypes about the sexual promiscuity of LGBTTQ people may lead students to be wary of others they "suspect" of being queer in change rooms. Stereotypes equating sexual predation and homosexuality cause people to fear victimization unnecessarily and to police spaces where they feel vulnerable. Lack of adult oversight can increase feelings of vulnerability.

Bullies may feel they can get away with harassing behaviour in change rooms because teachers are not there to intervene. In addition, students who are harassed or who see others bullied in change rooms may fail to report those instances to teachers. Even when they do, teachers might refuse to intervene. Educators may avoid entering change rooms with their students for fear of raising questions about their own sexuality or alleged sexual misconduct. For instance, Lindsay Willow, a teacher and lesbian in Nova Scotia, was criminally investigated for the alleged sexual abuse of a female student in 2006 after they left a change room together. The false accusation was instigated by a co-worker and the allegation was investigated despite the student involved denying any foul play.

Although she kept her job, Willows' employers barred her from extra-curricular activities that involved time alone with students. Fearing that this legal determination would undermine her career, Willow brought a complaint to the Nova Scotia Human Rights Tribunal. The tribunal members concluded that Ms. Willow's sexual orientation was a significant factor in the false accusations. She received an apology and a retraction of all accusations from school board officials and was awarded an unprecedented $27,375 in damages (*Lindsay Jane Willow v. Halifax Regional School Board* 2006). While the tribunal members identified homophobia as an underlying motivation for the accusations, surely cases like this must make even straight teachers reluctant to enter change rooms where students are present.

Not all volunteers in this study described their experiences in change rooms as negative. For example, Nadeem said:

> I didn't find it awkward! I have no complaints in that department!... I find if you show confidence in who you are and what you were doing, I found

> the attacks, if there were any, to be non-existent.... I'm gay, so what, I'm going to change with all you other guys. Too bad if you don't like it, go somewhere else. This is my space too. (gay, male)

Nadeem openly resisted homophobia and transphobia. He attributed these experiences to his growing self-confidence, popularity and school involvement. Nadeem said that having an older, overprotective brother at his high school probably helped, yet he knew that less fortunate queer students at his school were "made fun of... constantly" (gay, male). He believed that queer youth were most likely harassed on off-school property during lunch breaks or on their way to and from school. Nadeem was frequently hit with snowballs on his walks home. The following quotations illustrate his and others' experiences:

> I was walking home and someone threw an orange at me. So I picked up the orange, 'cause it landed on my backpack, and I chucked it back at them. And, I don't think it hit them. And then once I got snowballed [see quotation at beginning of this section]. So those were like the two, worst violent acts that ever happened to me, so, you know, not so bad. (Nadeem, gay, male)

> We were walking home one day... and they started screaming things, drove around the block and came back, beat him up, I was like, "What the fuck?" So I had to call an ambulance.... (Jamie, queer/gay, *)

Almost one-quarter of the young people experienced physical violence based on their sexual orientation or gender identity. They insisted that school staff rarely addressed the underlying homophobia and transphobia in physical harassment. We were told that teachers usually react to physical assaults they witness; however, there is a tendency to treat the incidents as general bullying. In other words, while staff members challenge physical behaviour, they fail to address the homophobia or transphobia that underpins it, sending the message that the attitude (HTP) is acceptable but that the manifestation (physical violence) is not. Failing to address insidious homophobic and transphobic expressions may explain why subtler manifestations persist.

Subtle Harassment

Given the tendency of school administrators, academics and the media to focus on spectacular forms of bullying at the expense of other, more subtle forms, there is a danger of assuming that less visible manifestations of homophobic and transphobic bullying in schools are a non-issue. According to participants in this study, HTP harassment persists in these forms of everyday harassment.

Dominant definitions and assumptions fuel students' perceptions of what constitutes bullying and can cause youth to downplay non-violent forms of harassment. For example, most of the young people we spoke with immediately downplayed their experiences or questioned whether they could be classified as "bullying." Asked what types of homophobic or transphobic incidents came to mind when reflecting on their high-school years, several of them qualified their experiences, saying that they didn't suffer physical violence and that their experiences were not "that bad":

> High school for me wasn't really typified by bullying.... Although I was bullied on some occasions because people perceived that I was queer it wasn't like really severe, you know, beatings or... that kind of thing. (Sam, queer/gay, queer)

> I didn't really have any bad experiences come to mind... but now that I think about it... (Xin, gay, gay)

Discussing HTP harassment in a group format, however, participants adjusted their concepts of bullying in relation to others' experiences. Talking about HTP bullying may have lead participants to view what were once seen as innocuous kinds of homophobia and transphobia as serious bullying or, alternatively, to downplay them depending on other participants' experiences with bullying. For example, after hearing Haley recount how a teacher told her she was going to "burn in Hell," Phoenix expressed disbelief about the level of HTP harassment that went on in that high school:

> I... have such a hard time visualizing that, like I don't want to invalidate your experience at all 'cause I'm sure it totally was that way, but in my mind, the idea of a teacher telling me that I would burn in Hell would be the kind of thing I could get them fired for! (queer, androgynous)

The focus group environment also encouraged participants to reframe their high school experiences and to identify some as homophobic or transphobic when they might not have otherwise. After hearing about subtle forms of HTP from other people in the group, Xin said:

> Now that I think about it... I just think there were small little things, like we tried to set up a GSA [Gay-Straight Alliance] and we put posters around, and like a week later people had tore them down and we had to

put them back up. Or like writing over what we wrote and then we had to take them down and put up new ones. (gay, gay)

In general, participants were eventually able to express how non–physically violent forms of harassment affected them. Nevertheless, their narratives illustrate that students and teachers may tacitly accept these modes because of perceptions that subtle HTP is "not that bad." In group discussions, all felt that their former schools had a homophobic or transphobic atmosphere, were not entirely queer-friendly, and that harm did not always manifest as physical injury.

Ten of the sixteen young people recalled incidents where they or someone else they knew who was LGBTTQ experienced *direct* forms of verbal harassment. These participants, or others perceived to be LGBTTQ, were called a derogatory name or singled out when classmates "outed" them as LGBTTQ.

There was one guy... I guess I dressed kind of differently... and in my wisdom I decided that it would be really cool to buy a plaid shirt. Like a plaid flannel shirt. And of course I didn't know at the time that that's... total 80s lesbian garb or whatever. But... he knew. I don't know how he knew but he's like, "Oh my god you're such a dyke!" (Sam, queer/gay, queer)

People, usually people who had pretty low self-confidence themselves, I thought, would try [to] "out" me or stuff like that or just like name-calling.... And then in senior high... my best friend kind of turned on me I guess... it was almost daily name-calling or just putting me down or whatever. (Corey, gay, male)

Nadeem: There was still the random homophobic slurs that I endured.... Heather: Did anyone directly call you queer? (*, female)
Nadeem: Well, a few, but like, I'd be walking in the hall and I'd hear "faggot" or "homo." (gay, male)

There was this one kid... he was constantly coming up to me in the hallways, "Are you gay?" "I know you're gay!" "Are you gay?"... he just kept attacking me about it.... Later on when I finally did come out... I kind of looked back at that and was like, well I guess I always was, but why couldn't he just walk away? Why did he always have to ask? (Xander, gay/homosexual, male)

There was one guy who always called me a faggot and stuff. I didn't really think much of it, because he wasn't really that hard core mean about it, he would just be like, you know, "Hey faggot," or whatever, or like, "Oh, you're gay aren't you?" and I'd just kind of ignore it. (Trevor, gay, male)

Although some said they were not affected much by HTP comments, often these experiences were the first examples of HTP that they recalled. Even those who said they were not deeply affected by such comments felt that verbal harassment has some negative impact. Certainly, there was consensus that these experiences constituted a form of homophobia or transphobia. Participants were not able to come to such a consensus in regards to less direct uses of terms associated with queer identities.

Participants recalled how insults were used to put down people or objects not actually perceived as LGBTTQ. Barbed words like "gay," "queer" or "fag" are used to insult other students, regardless of one's perceived sexual orientation or gender identity. Children often use these terms before knowing what they actually mean (Blumenfeld and Raymond 1993). Labels associated with queer identities are used to belittle people, but also to describe anything that is perceived as undesirable (i.e., "that's so gay"). Used in this manner, these terms may be seen as indirect forms of verbal HTP, which participants identified as rampant. Even when interviewees did not share their own experiences of hearing homophobic and transphobic insults, they nodded in agreement with what others said.

Actually it happened all the time. I don't know... it's just the... words friends use sometimes, you know, like "don't be a fag" or "that was faggy" or whatever. But yeah it was everywhere. (Ethan, gay, male)

I think the whole, "that's gay" was still common and still went on in the classroom and the teachers still didn't do anything about it. (Xin, gay, gay)

Although there is a movement to "reclaim" words such as fag, queer, dyke and homo, they still hold negative connotations and are insulting because of their use as HTP pejoratives. Yet, the use of labels associated with queer and trans identities may not always be taken as harmful. In his study of college-aged heterosexual youth who called friends names like "fag," Burn (2000) found that half of the participants used such terms to gain social acceptance and did not see them as homophobic putdowns. In our study, the dialogue concerning discourse or language in school revealed a disconnect between phrases such as "that's so gay" and homosexual or transgender identities. In response to another group member's experiences with direct HTP name-calling, Phoenix said:

> People who got called faggot weren't actually perceived as being gay, it was just the insult word.... They don't actually think you're gay, they just don't... really know what the word "fag" means. (queer, androgynous)

Participants disagreed about two issues here: first, whether HTP slurs were truly harmful, and second, whether they should intervene when they heard them. Some participants thought phrases such as "that's so gay" were harmful to queer people, especially when they went unchallenged. One person believed that straight youth may not be aware of the power of the language they use, but for some queer youth, the same words can have catastrophic effects. Referring to a former girlfriend who committed suicide because of homophobia from peers and family, Jamie said:

> They don't really pay attention whenever they hear about someone... or when they hear someone say "oh that's just so gay" or whatever, and for them it just goes totally out of their mind but for me it's like, "Well that's the same words that killed my girlfriend" kind of thing so, you never know. (queer/gay, *)

Sam lamented that teachers "would rarely admonish people for calling others fag" and was especially troubled by one experience:

> There was this kid who was saying "Don't call me gay," "I'm not gay," and then [other kids] are like, "Yeah, you're gay, you're gay." And I'm just like, "Okay, that's not a cool thing.... In this school we don't insult people based on their sexual orientation...." And then the teacher actually intervened at that point, he was like "Just let it go." In front of the students like, "Just don't blow this out of proportion," you know, "Boys will be boys." So I was like, what the hell? That sort of flies in the face of... the school standards or whatever. (queer/gay, queer)

Some participants found that phrases such as "that's so gay" were used so frequently that it would be impossible to intervene all of the time. Others saw HTP pejoratives as inoffensive and thought we should focus on more serious forms of harassment. The following excerpts are from three different discussion groups in which people said they use phrases such as "that's so gay":

> Trevor: I thought it was funny that there was one of my friends who was... hardcore like, "No, you can't say that's gay!" and all this stuff.... I don't really care if someone says that. Because I know they're not directing it at anybody.

Narrah: I say it all the time. (pansexual, female)

Trevor: Yeah, you say it a lot. I'm okay with that, I don't think that's such a bad thing, because I know it's just a stupid comment.... It's not really pointing out anybody... it's not like the "throw them in a bag and throw them off a truck" or something. That's a little more intense, but I don't mind that one so much.... I know it's still bad, because it's like a stereotype, or a derogatory term, but I don't think that's as bad as the others that are there. I could deal with that if that's all I heard in high school, is "that's so gay!" (gay, male)

Like, you know they don't mean it. But I don't know.... I sometimes say "that's gay." (Ethan, gay, male)

See, I started using that word a lot in high school.... If you're going to do that to me, it doesn't bother me so much, I know what I am! Let's give it to you and see how you like it. So my friends started calling me straight and I'm like, "I hate you all!" (Haley, lesbian/queer, female)

This use of "gay" and other terms might be a result of mainstream influences, but could also be a way to reclaim the terms. For example, because Haley proudly identified as a lesbian or queer, she said she was not bothered much by people's intended insults. In other words, she was likely bothered more that someone was trying to insult her than by the actual term used in the attempt. Knowing that levels of HTP were high in her school, she found using homophobic pejoratives herself to be an effective way to aggravate her classmates. Haley stated that she was more upset when her friends called her "straight" than when others would call her gay. This tack seemed to be one way of removing stigma or reframing LGBTTQ identities.

Young people heard explicitly HTP comments in their own classrooms and also read them on the walls of their high schools. Although graffiti is not a direct form of verbal harassment, many of the same phrases hurled at queer youth are etched on bathroom walls and other school property. Graffiti can send general messages that queer people are not welcome (Smith 1998). In our study, three participants noted that promotional materials for the Gay-Straight Alliances (GSAs) at their high schools were vandalized with HTP writing. Earlier in this chapter, Xin (gay, gay) discussed how his GSA posters were torn down or written on. Nadeem said that HTP remarks were written on his student election posters. Trystan mentioned graffiti in the change room.

There would be stuff written about me in the change room.... It was mainly written on the bathroom walls. And occasionally I had stuff written on my locker in the change room. (gay, male)

Teachers may not see graffiti or, when they do, they may dismiss is as a case of mere vandalism rather than recognizing it as a form of homophobia or transphobia. Queer youth get the message loud and clear. Smith (1998, 320) says that graffiti is "a form of public speech but with a permanence lacking in speech." Another form of verbal harassment often downplayed is gossip.

Surprisingly, participants spent little time talking about gossip as a form of harassment they faced, although some of the exclusionary tactics discussed later may have been coupled with gossip. In other studies, researchers have noted that up to 87 percent of students reported hearing negative rumours about them at school (Kosciw et al. 2008). Sam spoke of the power of gossip, sharing an experience in which another student started a rumour that Sam and a female friend were dating but were not open about their relationship because they were insecure about their homosexuality. This, despite the fact that Sam's friend was in a heterosexual relationship at the time:

Some girl started a rumour that [I was dating my best friend].... [My best friend] was dating somebody that that girl wanted to date... so [the girl] started this rumour that [my best friend] went out with [him] because she was insecure about her sexuality and was trying to throw them off. (queer/gay, queer)

For the most part, however, participants did not relay experience with gossip. The most obvious explanation for the few experiences with gossip is that we tend to focus on dramatic forms of harassment at the expense of subtle manifestations. Perhaps participants did not remember or even know of rumours about them.

Other instances where indirect HTP comments were made (comments not directed at someone perceived as LGBTTQ) involved the expression of personal viewpoints on homosexuality while in a school setting. Five people mentioned incidents when classmates or teachers made unmistakable, often religious-based homophobic or transphobic comments under the guise of expressing a personal viewpoint. As discussed in Chapter Three, several people mentioned social conservatism and religion when citing factors that they believed contributed to HTP in their high schools. Haley recalled at least two occurrences where teachers condemned her sexuality using religious arguments. The first incident, when she was told she would "burn in Hell," was mentioned earlier. In the second incident,

> We had an English sub [substitute teacher] come in, like, high prissy, churchgoing Roman Catholic.... I was doing a project on gay and straight differences at the time, for Comparative Civilizations... and she reads it and takes it away. And I'm like, "I need my homework back, please." And she's like, "No, God doesn't respect what you're doing." (lesbian/queer, female)

Such overt HTP statements made by teachers were rare. Classmates, however, sometimes made offensive comments in front of instructors.

> Just like, more of a general statement would be made. I remember one kid... somehow we got on the topic of gays and he said, "Oh, all of them should be put in a bag and thrown off the back of a truck." It wasn't talking about me, but he was just talking about gays in general. So, you know, it bothered me, but it wasn't like, hey, [I] should be... put in a bag and thrown off the back of a truck. (Nadeem, gay, male)

> We got off topic about abortion, and also gay marriage and all that kind of stuff. It basically boiled down to me and this dude friend of mine, and then these prep girls... it just became an ongoing battle. And the thing that pissed me off the most is that, they say they're Christian girls, yet they're wearing the short shorts or whatever, and they're saying that gay people don't deserve to have the sanction of marriage. (Heather, *, female)

> Something about gay men came up and one student was like, "I hate all gay people. I wish they would all die." And the teacher... basically just ignored it.... She said... with a smile... "Well, we shouldn't really say things like that in class." But she was smiling the whole time. So, she really didn't help at all. (Corey, gay, male)

Homophobic and transphobic sentiments expressed under the guise of presenting one's views on homosexuality or transgenderism may seem harmless to many people but can be especially harmful to the queer youth who are present.

Speaking about anti-queer hate propaganda, Faulkner (2007, 65) details the tensions between "those who argue for the right to freedom of hate speech and expression and those who argue for the rights of groups to be protected from speech that promotes hatred." Perhaps these tensions play into teachers' tolerance of HTP comments in classrooms. Allowing one person to express their negative views, though, may make it difficult for others to express their sexuality and gender or at least to do so safely (Faulkner 2007). Teachers' decisions not to intervene may also be based on an assumed absence of queer people in schools.

Students and teachers likely express negative opinions about homosexuality and transgenderism under an assumed absence of queer people. Such comments make it difficult for queer youth to come out and reinforce assumptions about the heterosexuality and gender conformity of students. It is not surprising, then, that the former students rarely made any rejoinder to those who were making the comments. Feeling extremely unwelcome and upset by hateful statements were among the reasons given for their inaction. Conversely, some said such comments did not affect them much because they were not directed at them personally (e.g., see Nadeem's statement above).

In any case, participants identified assumptions about students' sexualities and gender identities as a significant problem in high schools that lead to both direct and indirect verbal forms of HTP. In some cases queer identities were recognized in schools, and this recognition obviously made other people uncomfortable. Discomfort with queer youth sometimes resulted in avoidance, exclusion or other interpersonal forms of harassment.

For instance, Narrah, a pansexual female, discussed two instances where others in her high school avoided or segregated queer youth:

> We had a cooking club, and it was basically all of my friends who were all gay, obviously, or bi, and it was our turn to do cafeteria lunch, and normally, cafeteria lunches are everyone's lined up forever for most of lunch just to get the food, and it was a really slow lunch. And I overheard people in the hallways afterwards being like, "Oh, we're going to get AIDS 'cause they're all gay," and all this stuff. And I was just like, "Whoa!... We're cooking the food, we're not having sex with it!"... That really bothered me, because, you know, we worked so hard, and just because we were not straight, most of the school didn't want to come eat and even the teachers [avoided the meals]. It was that bad!

> We did a fast at the school, like a famine, and... [the teachers] were like dividing the kids to go into the separate gyms to sleep, because we spent the night in the school and the teachers like, "Okay, you, you, you, this one, you, you, you, this one," and [the queer youth] all got like singled out. And got stuck on the end by ourselves.... This was the teacher! Right? So, it's like, I don't know, like between the students and the teachers at my school... it sucked. It did suck really bad.

In Narrah's experience, students made explicit links between homo-sexuality and Acquired Immune Deficiency Syndrome (AIDS), and teachers made veiled references to contagiousness and sexual aggressiveness. Angelides (2005, 275) sees the classification of homosexuality itself and the various negative assumptions that have come along with that classification as the product of "the broader process of medicalization of sexual deviance, which began from the nineteenth century to catalogue the various departures from procreative sexuality according to distinct types, species, or psychic identi-ties of sexuality." Aside from being seen as diseased, students and teachers in Narrah's and others' experiences portrayed queer people as sexual preda-tors. Faubert and Haskell (2006) observed the frequent equation of sexual offending, specifically pedophilia, with homosexuality by criminal justice staff and society at large. This phenomenon was especially apparent in sex crime panics involving children in Canada during the 1930s, 1950s and again in the 1990s.

In the 1990s, the media publicized several stories about sexual abuse of children in Ontario, including the London, Ontario, "kiddie porn ring" and the Maple Leaf Gardens scandal (Maynard 2001). Maynard (2001, 84) claims that media coverage of these events "transform men who break the law ('sexual offenders') into men with distinct types of sexual identities ('predatory homosexuals' and 'pedophiles')." Freedman (1987, 103) has noted that media representatives and academics have historically used the terms "sex criminal, pervert, psychopath, and, homosexual" interchangeably. More recently, Faulkner drew on a report by Hess (as cited in Faulker 2007, 70–71), to detail several harmful misconceptions about homosexuality promoted through North American media, including:

> views about the depravity of homosexuals; the belief that gays spread disease and sickness and the promotion of AIDS as a ho-mosexual disease; the view that queers are dangerous and pose a security risk; the view that gay and lesbian persons are highly sexed and sexually deviant; and finally, the suggestion is made that gay and lesbian persons conspire to destroy social institutions such as the family and thus destroy society as a whole. (Faulkner 2007, 70–71)

Such misinformation in popular media and scholarship shapes perceptions of homosexuality and sometimes presents LGBTTQ people as having uncontrol-lable sexual urges that would lead them to "hit on" anyone regardless of their sexual orientation or age. Ideas about sexual voraciousness and contagion may lead students to avoid those perceived as LGBTTQ. According to one participant (and Narrah above), some students did just that.

> For me, it tended to be the girls. I would hang out with the guys and I'd be just one of the guys and the girls would be like, "Eeuww, I don't want to be near you; you might want to get in bed with me." (Jamie, queer/gay, *)

Not only did classmates avoid being in proximity to queer youth, they also avoided openly supporting them.

> The student council was... supposed to announce everything, like what's going on [in] school today, you know? And I guess you could tell that maybe they weren't so comfortable saying, "Oh there's a Gay-Straight Alliance today." (Sam, queer/gay, queer)

There are several reasons why students and teachers may be uncomfortable speaking about queer people and issues that affect them. First, they may be unsure of the correct terminology to use and worry about offending others. Second, terms associated with queer identities are often only heard in negative contexts in schools. This may lead people to feel that they are saying "bad" words by using labels associated with queer identities. Still others may be uncomfortable showing support for LGBTTQ people for fear of being perceived as queer themselves (Edwards 2006). Whatever the reason, the former students believed that "discomfort" with queer people needed to be dealt with before outright homophobic and transphobic behaviours could be addressed.

In their day-to-day experiences, students did not see queer people or issues affecting them reflected in their school environment. The young people we spoke with felt that their high schools were not completely supportive of LGBTTQ people. Similarly, Nayak and Kehily (1996) speak of the "everyday-ness" of homophobia in North American schools. They, as did participants in this study, draw attention to the lack of LGBTTQ people in school curriculum. Marinoble (1998, para. 3) refers to this absence as "the blind spot in the school mirror." Describing this analogy, Marinoble (1998, para. 3) explains: "When driving an automobile, a blind spot can be very dangerous. When looking at oneself, a blind spot can have serious consequences." In this study, participants identified silence about queer people on the part of school staff and in the curriculum as a significant factor that produced the HTP they experienced.

Not only did the youth feel there was a lack of discussion about queer people in their high schools, but some were actually silenced by administrators when they attempted to break that silence. For example, two people, both from rural, conservative towns, had their attempts to form a GSA thwarted by school administrators.

> I started up a GSA at my school, couldn't get a teacher to help. Had to blackmail my principal to do it.... I got [a school board official's] number....

I went in there and said if you don't do it, I'll phone her up.... I had the...
Counsellor's help. But, that's about it... no teacher would lend a room....
They wouldn't be around it. They wouldn't help because it would cause
too much issues. (Haley, lesbian/queer, female)

Like other subtle forms of HTP, silence about, and silencing of, queer
youth creates heterosexist and gender-limiting high-school environments
where sexualities and gender identities outside of the mainstream are over-
looked (Burn 2000; Meyer 2006; Pascoe 2007). These environments encourage
young people to see LGBTTQ people as unfamiliar, if not unnatural, and lead
to more overt forms of homophobia and transphobia. As stated earlier, subtle
forms of HTP, including silence about LGBTTQ people, often go unrecognized
and, even when recognized, are frequently not addressed by school staff or
students.

Subtle Harassment: Context

Subtle harassment often happened on school premises and sometimes in front
of teachers. Due to school administrators' emphasis on physical harassment,
subtle forms are usually treated less seriously and ignored or downplayed
by students, educators and administrators. By condoning, for example, the
pejorative use of words such as "gay," educators bolster negative attitudes
toward LGBTTQ people.

School staff are restricted from meting out corporal punishment, but
participants noted that they sometimes engage in subtle forms of homophobia and transphobia. These actions teach students that homosexuality and
gender variance are unnatural or, in one participant's words, simply "wrong."
Students may engage in HTP behaviours as a way to enforce boundaries
between what they learn is "right" (heterosexuality and gender conformity)
and "wrong" (homosexuality and gender variance), and to punish wrongdo-
ers (Lombardi et al. 2001). The techniques a young person uses to enforce
heterosexuality and gender conformity may vary according to whether or
not a teacher is present, and also by gender of the bully.

Several researchers argue that bullying methods vary by gender, with
males choosing more direct and physical techniques and females, more subtle
and indirect forms (Walton 2006). Some participants agreed with this. Asked
who was most likely to physically assault a queer person, Phoenix answered:

Guys. Guys. Males. I found that any homophobic comments I heard from
females were, kind of, it was more like gossip. It wasn't... vicious, not in the
same way.... They wouldn't attack you directly, they might talk about you
behind your back and it would be kind of quiet but with like physical or
aggressive situations it was always males. (queer, androgynous)

In addition to their penchant for direct forms of harassment, group participants said that males were generally more likely to engage in HTP bullying in the first place. It is possible, though, that females engage in just as much bullying as males but use more subtle forms. For example, one person said that even females who did not intend to be homophobic or transphobic could say upsetting things:

> I don't want to really say that it was homophobic. Some girls would be like "Oh," you know, "he's feminine" or something like that, so... I don't know if it was really hurtful, but... it did affect me at the time. (Corey, gay, male)

Another person disagreed with the assertion that females' intentions were benign:

> I was bullied really badly in elementary school.... I went to high school and wanted sort of a fresh start. In the first week I was sitting in the cafeteria with some of my friends, and just to give you an idea at this point I was pretty chunky and I was, well, masculine. So we were just... sitting at the lunch table and there was some Grade 10s.... One of them dared the other one to hit on me I guess.... It was, so clear that it wasn't like "oooh" [a real attraction] right? (Sam, queer/gay, queer)

Tentatively, our research implicates males as key harassers of queer high-school youth. Kenway and Fitzclarence (1997) attribute males' proclivity for violence in schools to attempts to claim, or at least adhere to, hegemonic masculinity (a term discussed in Chapter One and in the glossary). Criminologists and sociologists such as Connell (2005), Kimmel (1994; Kimmel and Mahler 2003) and Messerschmidt (2007; Connell and Messerschmidt 2005) have started to deconstruct how the ideal of hegemonic masculinity can undermine high-school boys, but the findings from our exploratory research indicate that there is more work to be done. Still, we heed Walton's (2006, 48) caution that "not even researchers on bullying are immune from seeing and interpreting human behaviour through what Devor (1989) calls a dominant gender schema." If females engage in subtle forms of HTP more than males, we may downplay females' involvement in HTP bullying as a result of our tendency to focus on physical forms of harassment. Regardless of who they were being bullied by, some participants thought they were able to challenge the heterosexist and gender-limiting nature of their high-school environments and, in turn, to affect levels of subtle and overt HTP harassment.

Resistance to HTP

Group participants made it clear that they were not merely passive victims of HTP in their high schools; they found various ways of coping with the harassment and of pushing back against HTP bullying. For example, participants often responded to HTP bullying with humour, which may have served both as a coping mechanism and as a tool to convey that they had not been affected by the homophobia and transphobia they experienced. Participants also used humour in recounting their high-school experiences with the group.

After sharing a story about their friend being beaten unconscious, Jamie smirked and assured us, "He fought well, though!" Similarly, although Nadeem acknowledged that his being pelted with snowballs and oranges and homophobic slurs was definitely homophobic or transphobic harassment, he responded to these incidents, both at the time and in sharing his experiences, with sarcasm and humour, often laughing as he spoke with us in the group. It is difficult to know whether participants such as Jamie and Nadeem genuinely see their experiences as comical or whether they have adopted humour as a means of coping with past HTP encounters whose initial impact was more negative.

Although humour may have been adopted by participants as a defence to HTP bullying, many of the young people seemed to frame their use of witty comebacks and sarcasm as tools of resistance to hamper perpetrators' efforts to position LGBTTQ as denigrated identities. For example, Haley, who identified as lesbian or queer female, used humour to deflect others' attempts to belittle her. She laughed as she said:

> One kid was getting threatened and punched.... They were pushing him and punching him... and calling him fag, and gay, and everything, and I stepped in between and pushed him out and said, "You're gonna call someone gay? Call me, I am! You gonna hit me? Do it now!" And he hit me. [RH: Did he?] Yeah, I kind of deserved it.... I told him that he shouldn't get mad, that I did his girlfriend last night. (lesbian/queer, female)

There were several examples where Haley also used witty comebacks when she felt denigrated because of her sexual orientation. When a teacher warned her that being a lesbian would lead her to "burn in Hell," Haley replied, "That's okay, I started Fed Ex'ing my stuff [to Hell] years ago" (lesbian/queer, female). The same teacher refused to help Haley on an exam until "she learned to love Jesus." Haley, who was deeply involved with the Christian community at the time, told the teacher that she was indeed "tight" with Jesus and that he did not approve of the teacher's reproaches (in her words, "He says you suck.").

Other means of resistance were also mentioned by the young people. For example, frustration with HTP harassment can lead queer youth to respond physically. Some participants recalled reacting violently to non-violent HTP harassment by peers and even teachers. One person said that he would often respond physically to HTP harassment because he had "a violent temper" (gay, male). Demetrius used physical violence to push back against homophobia or transphobia.

> Demetrius: There was this one guy that I really didn't like during football. He was pretty much the worst when it came to all the guys. He was always making homo comments... that gets pretty much any gay guy pretty steamed when their football teammates are friggin' talking about something that is important to their personal life, right? So, friggin', I was on [the] defensive line... and [the] guy... was on the offence and I... went right for him and put him right on the ground as hard as I fucking could.... I put my shoulder pads right into his gut, and that's part of you that's not padded.
> Xander: I just don't think you should use violence as a solution! (gay/homosexual, male)
> Demetrius: Well, I know it's not a solution, but it sure made me feel better! The guy could hardly breathe for the rest of practice. (gay, male)

Earlier, Demetrius mentioned that he did not like to resort to violence in response to HTP harassment. Here, however, he seized the opportunity to legitimately engage in physical violence in reaction to a teammate's homophobic comments. Illustrating again that he sometimes responded to HTP with physical violence, Demetrius said, "The last time I saw something written on a locker I caved the locker in with my foot" (gay, male).

Haley explained how she reacted to ongoing homophobic comments made by one of her instructors:

> I fought.... I got angry and I yelled at her. I threw a chair at her once. (lesbian/queer, female)

Haley went on to say that when she experienced HTP in high school, she would "get mad and have tantrums… flip out." In fact, Haley said she became known as a bully in high school because she was in so many fights. She saw her role in the altercations as defensive and described herself as being in an "us or them" situation. By far, Haley recounted the most instances of harassment, both at the hands of teachers and other students. Even she, though, was able to identify positive experiences in her high-school years.

Positive High-School Experiences

Despite feeling as though their schools were generally heterosexist or gender limiting, three young people described their high-school experiences as positive and felt supported by at least some school staff and friends. One participant (Xin) told group members that he was comfortable enough among his peer group to come out in Grade 9: a timing that other study participants thought was especially early compared to their own experiences. Reliving some positive aspects of high school, this participant said:

> The only experiences in high school that made me... who I am today is just my friends being there when I came out to them or whatever. And also, I don't want to... say this, but... I guess possibly being Asian, like word doesn't get around as much, I guess?... It sort of just stayed in our own group..... And I guess that's why not everyone knew. But I didn't really care who knew anyway. I was fine with everyone knowing, or not knowing. (Xin, gay, gay)

In this case, Xin attributed his positive experience, in part, to the ethnicity of his peer group. Interestingly enough, this was the only time participants mentioned ethnicity as a factor in HTP bullying, aside from comparisons of how students and staff react to and address racism and HTP differently in schools. The second participant who had positive high-school experiences attributed this to a supportive staff member and the urban setting of the school.

Phoenix said that time in high school was unique because it was "fairly positive overall":

> For me, the first thing I thought of was a teacher that I had... he was openly gay.... It was his idea to found our school's GSA.... He was so supportive, he was always there to listen, he was always there to back me up on anything, so I just thought of him. (queer, androgynous)

Explaining why staff members in that high school were so supportive of LGBTTQ students, Phoenix said:

> I think that it helped a lot to have teachers who came from that... urban background. And had been dealing with, I mean, gay issues in the newspaper or around in the community.... And... having an instructor at my school in kind of his own way, kind of a gay activist, I think that that would have helped at any school, just to have that kind of instructor there. (queer, androgynous)

Certainly, supportive adults play a significant role in preventing HTP bullying and in moderating its effects. Espelage, Aragon, Birkett and Koening (2008) found that queer students who had supportive teachers and parents reported less depression, suicidal ideation and substance abuse than those who did not. Darwich (2008) has linked supportive adults to reduced levels of school truancy and alcohol abuse.

The third participant who said his high school experiences were generally positive described himself as "lucky" for his limited encounters with HTP bullying. Nevertheless, he mentioned homophobic and transphobic behaviour in his high school, some of it aimed at him. He attributed his overall positive experiences to his social position as well as to his own efforts to create a safe place for LGBTTQ youth in his high school. Comparing his experiences to those of other youth in the discussion group, Nadeem explained:

> I was really lucky in my high school because I have an older brother, a protective older brother.... But, I was lucky because I was popular, not to gloat, but I was well known, and everyone knew who I was. You know, "Oh, that's the gay kid." Maybe I was known for the wrong reasons, but I was known.... I was very involved, so that really helped a lot.... But, in the midst of all that, there was still like, the random homophobia slurs that I endured. But it wasn't bad. (gay, male)

Discussion groups encourage comparisons and redefinitions of bullying. For example, in contrast to other participants, Nadeem believed that his popularity and the presence of an older sibling at his school created a less hostile environment for him. However, Nadeem also felt that he played an active role in creating a safe environment for himself. For instance, he had no qualms about reporting students who had picked on him. He also provided his counsellors with resources for queer youth.

Other participants were able to recall positive experiences but did not feel that they could characterize their time in high school overall as very positive. Frequently, the youth talked about finding a group of supportive friends later on in high school. Asked why the bullying he experienced ended, Corey said:

> I think just not being around that friend anymore. And finding friends that... just saw me for who I was... I just had a really good, supportive group of friends. I was a lot more involved... in school and... I think it was more to do with me than it was with anyone else though. Like I had made the changes to surround myself with certain people. (gay, male)

In a separate group discussion, Xander expressed surprise at how well his fellow students reacted to his coming out:

It's funny, because when I finally did come out... almost everyone in my high school was like, "Oh, we already knew and we never cared." He [one person who bullied him] was the only one that ever had an issue with it. Like the only time that I really experienced homophobia in my high school was from him, one time. And that was it. And almost everyone I told about it was like that's really stupid.... I guess I really liked my high school. (gay/ homosexual, male)

Asked to come up with positive experiences related to their sexual orientation or gender identity in high school, all but one of the young people did so. These findings are consistent with research on positive experiences of queer youth in school (Darwich 2008; Varjas et al. 2007). It is clear that not all queer youth have completely negative experiences in high school, and some have rather positive experiences, even when they are out. It is impossible to know whether participants would have classified their experiences as positive if asked to do so during their high-school years. Over time, they may have reframed experiences they once saw as negative. The young people's current perceptions of their high-school experiences were important, though, as they shaped beliefs about how they were affected.

Few of the young people we spoke with experienced outright physical violence. Most recalled hearing insults — either as a general putdown or HTP sentiments made under the guise of expressing one's personal, sometimes religion-based, opinion. Still, there is a tendency among school staff and administrators to focus mostly on visible and physical forms of harassment. Narrow definitions of bullying leave the most frequent forms unaddressed, which can have a wide range of unhealthy consequences for queer youth.

Chapter 3

Outcomes and Origins of HTP

In the previous chapter, subtle forms of HTP were identified as being those most commonly experienced in the high schools. HTP harassment, however, no matter what the form, can have various effects on queer youth. Many youth in this study discussed the lasting impacts of HTP in high school. Still, some found ways to "rise above" (according to Nadeem) the harassment they faced. Certainly, youth who felt supported in their high school considered themselves better people for their experiences, but other participants did as well.

This chapter focuses on how people in our sample thought their high-school experiences with HTP affected them, regardless of whether the bullying was subtle or more overt. Participants were asked to reflect on how they were impacted while in high school and in the long term. In addition, the young people considered ways in which their high-school experiences, positive or negative, helped them in some way or resulted in a positive outcome. In some cases, such discussions helped the young people to reflect on their experiences in ways they might not have before. It also set an affirmative tone for the discussions and this work of exploring what can be a sombre subject.

Effects of HTP Bullying in High School

> One's reputation, whether false or true, cannot be hammered, hammered, hammered, into one's head without doing something to one's character. (Meyer and Dean 1998, 160)

As Meyer and Dean (1998) note in the above quotation, the pervasiveness of homophobia and transphobia (HTP) causes many youth to internalize negative attitudes toward lesbians, gay men, bisexuals, transgender, two-spirit, and queer (LGBTTQ) individuals before they begin to appreciate their own sexuality and/or gender. This kind of inward hatred or loathing is detrimental to everyone, but for youth who eventually identify as LGBTTQ, it has the potential to gravely affect their self-worth. Flowers and Buston (2001) claim that most adolescents who are minorities (e.g., ethnic minorities) can reduce distress through support from their families and peers. The minority status of LGBTTQ youth is not so obvious and is often not shared with family or friends. In fact, queer youth who choose to identify as LGBTTQ may be shunned by the people closest to them (Kitts 2005). Consequently, youth harassed because of their real or perceived sexual and/or gender identities frequently remain silent, failing to report the harassment they experience and its effects.

Participants in our study generally felt that HTP bullying created a need for self-censorship and was stifling in various ways. Most often this self-censorship resulted in the avoidance of gender nonconformity, thereby avoiding homophobic and transphobic accusations and accosting. Other young queer people have reported similar self-censorship effects (Mahan et al. 2006; Nayak and Kehily 1996; Smith 1998). For example, in Nova Scotia, Arsenault (2000) reported that the lesbians she interviewed believed they had to make themselves invisible to ensure their safety. Arsenault (2000, 1) asserted that "silence has surrounded the experiences of lesbians in the public school system. The presence of homophobia and heterosexism in this system has strengthened the silence, rendering lesbians invisible."

The young people we spoke with believed that even subtle forms of HTP induce youth to regulate their gender expressions so they will not be perceived as queer and consequently "picked on" (a term most participants used). For example, Sam believed that what some saw as a too-masculine appearance triggered insults such as "lezbo," and was "freaked out" that others read their appearance as queer at a point when they were perhaps unsure of their sexual orientation and gender identity. To avoid HTP harassment, Sam said that they were self-conscious about their appearance and the signals it gave off:

> It was terrible because... whenever I saw something I wanted to wear I had to interrogate myself and I'd be like, "Why do you want to wear this?" You know? Or like, "What will people think if you wear this?" I remember buying a pair of shoes, and we got them home and I had to take them back because I was like, "Oh my god!" you know, this is like... [signal of sexuality/gender identity] and they were just, they were shoes, right? And they weren't like big... dykey motorcycle boots or anything.
> RH: You changed the way you dressed so that people wouldn't...
> Sam: To an extent.... I guess I sort of started dressing like a slob, you know?... just sort of neutral.... If you saw that person you wouldn't be like, "Oh, well they're a gender terrorist." You'd be like, "Oh well they just are... a slob," you know, like they don't care. (queer/gay, queer)

Sam was limited in school-related activities. Physical activities that could be labelled as masculine were avoided, a decision that had consequences for their physical and mental health:

> Though I really wanted to sign up for the rugby team in high school I didn't because I thought that people would think that was too masculine

and call me a lesbian.... The paranoia about how I thought people would react to my appearance and activities with which I occupied my time I believe caused me to neglect my body, and to gain a lot of weight, which doubtlessly led to more body dysphoria. (queer/gay, queer)

Corey, on the other hand, said he had to be careful about how he spoke because of the tendency for people to associate soft or higher-pitched voices with effeminacy and, consequently, homosexuality. He said:

Overcoming that was tough because it's almost like it was silencing 'cause I didn't want to say anything. 'Cause people would try and identify [his sexuality] just [from] the way I spoke. So... it's taken me a long time, even public speaking or anything like that just from that, from those incidents, so... that sucked. (gay, male)

Corey credited a teacher who encouraged him to join the debate team with helping him to overcome his fear of public speaking.

In other discussion groups, Trevor, Narrah and Ethan also expressed feelings that HTP bullying in high school amounted to "silencing." Speaking of the immediate effects of their high-school experiences, they said:

Most of you people know me and know my personality and how crazy I can tend to be, but I wasn't that person in high school.... (Narrah, pansexual, female)

I guess I was kind of the same way because I was really shy in high school. I was so quiet I was like the random kid in the back of class and people probably didn't even know my name for half the year.... I didn't care though, I was just there to go to school and I preferred people to leave me alone, I liked being kind of invisible, kind of. Like I mean, if I had friends in the class I was okay, but if I didn't know anyone then I just kind of stuck to myself. (Trevor, gay, male)

It was pretty easy to, to get through high school, but, when you just say nothing, people will just think you're shy or whatever. (Ethan, gay, male)

Haley may not have been silenced entirely but she described "hiding" to avoid HTP harassment:

By the end [of high school] I just kind of hid. I was just like, "I don't want to deal with it." So I just stayed in [the] Drama room. (lesbian/queer, female)

Another person noted how awkward it was to have to hide his sexual orientation from his closest friends for fear of reprisals:

> Most of my friends from high school were actually really homophobic, and I never really told any of my friends that I am, you know, bi or anything, and none of them even really know to this day.... They've had discussions about how [homosexuality] is wrong, and I'll just kind of sit there and be like... "I'm not going to say anything." (Lukas, bisexual, male)

Jamie, whose story was especially moving, spoke of how queer youth may be doubly silenced by HTP bullying. To avoid being identified as LGBTTQ and subjected to HTP harassment, queer high-school students may become introverted, silent and uninvolved in their schools. Silenced or "closeted," queer youth are often unable to confide in others about the negative effects of HTP. Jamie, whose high-school girlfriend committed suicide, was unable to turn to others for support because they were "in the closet" at that time. Asked what experiences came to mind after reading an advertisement for the study, Jamie remembered:

> One of them was the experiences my ex-girlfriend had and that's still kind of touchy because she committed suicide. And so like that comes to mind initially and that [inaudible] could be an end result, and then... I remember being in high school and not being able to tell anyone because no one there knew and even now I'm not sure if anyone knows. (queer/gay, *)

Homophobic and transphobic messages communicated in schools can lead LGBTTQ youth to believe that their lives are worthless and expendable. Saewyc and her colleagues (2007) claim that suicide is the second leading cause of death among young people in Canada, and queer youth are over-represented among those who attempt to and those who successfully take their own lives. In a recent province-wide study in B.C., Saewyc et al. (2007, 31) reported that LGB youth in their sample were "significantly more likely to report suicidal thoughts in the past year compared to heterosexual peers." Queer youth attempted suicide at a rate of up to fives times as often as heterosexual youth (Saewyc et al. 2007). In an earlier study, researchers at the McCreary Centre Society found that nearly half of the seventy-seven lesbian and gay youth they surveyed in B.C. had attempted suicide, with the average age at attempt being thirteen (McCreary Centre Society 1999). Media reports and academic discussions of the suicides of Jamie Lazarre, an eighteen-year-old student from Prince George, and Hamed Nastoh, a fourteen-year-old Grade 8 student in Surrey, depict homophobic bullying as influential in their decision to end their lives.

In his meta-analysis of fifteen studies on suicide and queer youth, Kitts (2005, 623–24) reported that studies spanning the last twenty years consistently show that queer youth attempt suicide at twice the rate of heterosexual peers. Researchers across North America suggest that LGBTTQ individuals constitute approximately one-third of all youth suicides (Buston and Hart 2001; D'Augelli, Hershberger and Pilkington 2001; O'Connor 1995). That figure does not include unsuccessful suicide attempts by nearly half of all LGBTTQ youth (Wyss 2004). Still, researchers have discovered that youth who have social support are significantly less likely to think about suicide or engage in other risk-taking behaviours (Rutter 2007; Saewyc et al. 2006).

Unlike other participants who tended to avoid certain activities that might lead people to perceive them as LGBTTQ, Jamie actively engaged in behaviours that could cause others to assume they were heterosexual. Below, Jamie discusses how they sought to prove their heterosexuality to themselves and others:

> Because of all of it, I started trying to convince everyone else I was straight. And so I slept around a lot... and I wasn't sleeping around with girls, I was sleeping around with guys... to try to convince people that I was straight and that I liked it and stuff like that.... I spent a lot of time trying to get that into my brain like, "I do like guys, I do like guys." This is how I'm supposed to feel. (queer/gay, *)

Researchers in B.C. have found that queer youth report higher rates of pregnancy or of getting someone pregnant than heterosexual people of the same age (Saewyc et al. 2008). Aside from trying to prove one's heterosexuality, unsafe sexual practices that lead to pregnancy and sexually transmitted infections (STIs) may reflect sexual education programs in schools that "do not address the needs... or seem relevant to [the] social contexts" of LGBTTQ youth (Gay and Lesbian Medical Association 2001, 127). Radkowsky and Siegel (1997, 196) argue that queer youth may put themselves at risk of contracting STIs because they "do not care enough about their own well-being to practice safer sex." Still other queer youth may be at high risk for STIs because they have been forced out of their homes (Bochenek and Widney 2001; Burgess 1999; Kitts 2005). With few resources, some street-involved youth find themselves trading sex for food, shelter or money (Bochenek and Widney 2001; Gay and Lesbian Medical Association 2001; Trans Youth 2003).

In B.C., researchers at the McCreary Centre Society report that one in three street-involved females and one in ten of all street-involved youth they surveyed identified as lesbian, gay or bisexual (Smith et al. 2007). They confirmed that there were "a disproportionate number of gay, lesbian and bisexual youth who become street-involved or in other ways disenfranchised" and added that the number seems to be increasing (Smith et al. 2007, 15). In large U.S. cities, researchers find up to 40 percent of young homeless people identifying as LGB (Birden 2005; Bochenek and Widney 2001).

Apart from leaving home, some queer students may also stop attending school to avoid harassment (Bochenek and Widney 2001; Darwich 2008; D'Augelli 1998). Some of the youth we spoke with "hid" in their classrooms, trying not to draw attention to themselves. Others skipped classes or transferred schools to avoid bullying. In 2008 GLSEN reported that more than 30 percent of the queer youth they surveyed had skipped school in the prior month because they felt unsafe in the school environment compared to only 5 percent of heterosexual youth (Kosciw et al. 2008, 26). Some youth may drop out of school completely.

In a Philadelphia study, three out of four trans youth reported dropping out of high school. Most attributed this to harassment in school (Sausa 2005, 19). Sam spoke of a queer young woman who dropped out of school altogether because of HTP she experienced, combined with other challenges:

> Her learning disabilities and the instability in her life made it hard for her to keep up with school work and to attend classes so she made enemies with teachers. [She] burned some bridges with friends and the school and could not turn to her parents for support. By February of her Grade 11 year, [she] had dropped out of my high school, which was pretty much unheard of. (queer/gay, queer)

Negative effects, such as poor academic performance, can worsen the already stigmatized identities of LGBTTQ youth and increase the likelihood that they will suffer from depression and low self-esteem (Bochenek and Widney 2001; Saewyc et al. 2007; Wyss 2004). Speaking about the impact on their mental health, Jamie and Corey said:

> I went back in the closet for three years.... So needless to say that didn't do so well for my mental health. (Jamie, queer/gay, *)

> I think it was just my self-confidence in general, went down. And just like, the feeling of being on the outside all the time. (Corey, gay, male)

Some queer youth may react to HTP by denying their sexual or gender identity, and develop contempt for other minorities (including other LGBTTQ individuals) and themselves. DiPlacido (1998, 147) says that many queer youth take on negative messages about queer people and, realizing they differ from social norms, internalize homophobia and transphobia. Internalized homophobia and transphobia, DiPlacido (1998, 147) argues, "can range from self-doubt to overt self-hatred" and can lead to depression, self-mutilation, eating disorders and other long-term effects, including attempts at taking one's own life (see Dorias and Lajeunesse 2004 for more about young gay men and suicide).

Long-Term Impacts of HTP
Several participants believed experiences with homophobia and transphobia in high school were still impacting them and may continue to do so for some time. For example, many were left with fear that others would react negatively to their sexual orientation or gender identity.

> There's also the trust issue.... The combination of paranoia over negative reactions of people and feedback from my peers... made it so that I didn't trust many people to react kindly or even indifferently to my sexual orientation let alone to understand it. (Sam, queer/gay, queer)

> Even at [university] where it's so positive and embracing or whatever, [it's] still... hard for me.... Seeing a crowd in front of me, I still assume that there's people [who are] like who I went to high school with. (Corey, gay, male)

For some, rather than having trouble making new friends, existing friendships suffered. One person who described his friends as "really homophobic" could no longer spend much time with them:

> I guess it kind of pushed me away from my friends a little bit. You know, the fact that my friends were rather homophobic.... If I do see them when I'm in public, especially if I'm with my boyfriend or whatever, it's pretty awkward! Very awkward. But I haven't really let any of them know and, you know, I kind of feel fine keeping it that way just because of the way they are.... All my friends are really good friends, but they're just really close-minded people. (Lukas, bisexual, male)

Participants talked about how other queer youth struggling with HTP remarks had difficulty trusting people. Jamie had difficulties establishing a group for queer youth in a postsecondary educational institution. They noted how stigmatization of LGBTTQ people in high school influenced some young people's willingness to be involved:

> Even now, I'm trying to start up a [GSA] at [a college] and just seeing the amount of people that are interested in joining but don't want to have anything that could potentially connect them, like anything from walking

to a place where there's a meeting and they don't want to be seen there.... They're scared of that. And they're even scared to e-mail me just in case I might be able figure out who they are. And so that whole, just continuous shame coming back all over again, that can lead to so many different directions. (Jamie, queer/gay, *)

In general, participants described the immediate and long-term effects of experiencing HTP harassment in high school as involving a somewhat permanent, heightened air of caution and a censorship of signals that could be associated with queer identities. Yet, they discussed various ways their experiences with what could be seen as a crucible of HTP in high schools had positive outcomes as well.

Positive Outcomes

Varjas et al. (2007) and Savin-Williams (2005) criticize academics for over-emphasizing the negative effects of homophobic bullying at the expense of positive outcomes. Most queer youth we spoke to believed that their experiences helped them and others from their high school to grow. When asked about their experiences with HTP bullying, most immediately discussed negative effects. Haley, however, relayed positive outcomes first. This is especially interesting because she reported the most overt and severe HTP harassment of all the young people we interviewed. Speaking first about the effects of bullying on her and then about a sympathetic teacher in her school, Haley said:

[It] made me stronger.... Anyone can say anything to me now and I can be like, "Oh, whatever."... I'm just like, "I don't care, you're not worth my time."... Just shrug them off. It's not my fault they're scared, and I'm better looking.

I still go there [to her school].... I see my old teachers and one of my teachers... got me a Pride sticker... at this teacher conference... and she's got a "No Homophobia" sign posted in her classroom now because of me. (lesbian/queer, female)

Most participants did not speak of affirmation until they were specifically asked if their experiences with HTP had any positive outcomes. Not surprisingly, the young people who described their high-school experiences as generally positive were apt to recall affirmative outcomes without any prompting. Consider Xin, who came out to his peers in Grade 9:

The only experiences in high school that made me... who I am today, it's just my friends being there when I came out to them or whatever....

I remember being so scared just to tell them. But... from that point on I guess it became easier. (gay, gay)

Phoenix, whose experiences in high school were "generally very positive," was encouraged by supportive teachers and peers.

> I'd say it was a very positive effect... knowing... if there was any kind of gay bashing... I had resources to turn to. I always felt like I had support, like I would have legal support, like I would have emotional support.... It's helped me... accept myself really well. I think if I had a really, really negative experience I would have turned out... not as positive a person as I did.... I think it's helped me to realize also that I can help others too.... Seeing an instructor and administration and my friends support me then... when I was learning about myself and just kind of coming out and all that stuff... has helped me to support others. (queer, androgynous)

Several participants were motivated to help other queer youth as a result of their experiences with HTP in high school. Some even identified this desire as a motivation for taking part in our study. The final person who described his time in high school as generally positive mentioned how he became active in anti-homophobia initiatives and how that helped him:

> You know, I really believe in that phrase [taken from Nietzsche] "If it doesn't kill you, it's only going to make you stronger."... I kind of see myself as the phoenix and I rose! No, but I came above it. You know? I went above it and... that's what I feel you have to do. You can't let it get the best of you, or else you're just going to be down in the dumps and you're always going to be sad or upset about it. (Nadeem, gay, male)

Participants who did not feel their experiences were as positive as those mentioned above were still able to outline some benefits of HTP in high school. This usually involved feeling they had somehow matured.

> It... caused me to examine myself, my values, my motivations for acting, and other people's actions a lot so I feel that I know myself a lot better than a lot of people my age. I think my experiences have also made me be able to be more empathetic toward people. I also feel like I have something to prove to people — that I am not inferior — which I think motivates me to do well in school. (Sam, queer/gay, queer)

> Corey: I wouldn't have traded the experiences I had even if they were

bad because I think I really grew from them anyway. But, I mean, I think it would still be better if I didn't have to go through it at all. But I think I'm a lot stronger because of it and just for me to be able to share my experiences now and like maybe help someone.... I think that may be worth it.
RH: You said it helped you grow because of it, how do you think that is?
Corey: Just learning how to deal with problems and how not to deal with problems, especially. Because I realized that just being quiet and trying to ignore it didn't work.... I also realized how to be really independent and able to deal with things... on my own. So, it's made me independent but also realizing that there is a need to reach out to other people and that it is helpful to reach out. (gay, male)

You take people as they come.... You learn, when you go to places... people are going to be different. I've been to other small communities and they're fabulous. They're so nice, they don't care [that I'm a lesbian]... and you gotta take everyone for who they are, it doesn't matter. You gotta be positive about the world or else... no one will be.... I think, as horrible as my experiences are, they are positive. You know? I like the way I turned out, and I wouldn't of done it without 'em. (Haley, lesbian/queer, female)

I guess I figured by Grade 10, I didn't have to be afraid anymore, you know? Like it was as bad as it was gonna get, and I was just like screw it, I'm going to be open no matter where I am. People generally have more respect for me now. Because I'm open, rather than trying to act straight, saying "Oh, I had a girlfriend" when I really didn't. People never bought that. (Trystan, gay, male)

Sam noted that, although they had trouble trusting people they did not know well, existing friendships had become even stronger:

The positive effects of bullying I guess were that because I didn't trust a lot of people, the people I surround myself with now I feel that I can trust a lot. (queer/gay, queer)

Rivers (2004) reported that HTP bullying had positive outcomes for some of the 119 queer participants they interviewed. In their research, Rivers (2004, 174) found that "those who had been much more negatively affected by their experiences of bullying... [came] to terms with their sexual orientation much earlier" than youth who were less impacted. In our study, most participants were able to channel the oppressive power directed at them into more positive outcomes. While not unscathed, they did rise, as Nadeem put it, above their sometimes blistering experiences and emerged feeling more resilient.

Rooting Out HTP: Origins and Implications

The causes of and recommendations for the reduction of HTP often came up as a natural part of the participant discussions. If it did not surface, participants were asked to think about how homophobia and transphobia emerge in high schools. Three major themes participants identified as contributing to HTP in their high schools involved the regulation of gender norms, a lack of exposure to queer people and issues affecting them, and the natural maturation process.

Regulating Gender Roles

Prevailing stereotypes about queer people tend to depict gay men as "effeminate" and lesbians as "masculine" (Blumenfeld and Raymond, 1993; Meyer, 2007a). Heterosexuality, on the other hand, is often associated with traditional gender roles. It is no surprise, then, that young trans and gender-variant people are often perceived as queer and sometimes harassed (Bochenek and Widney 2001; Messerschmidt 2007; Varjas et al. 2007). Historically, gay men and lesbians have been stereotyped as "gender inverts." Consequently, youth who do not conform to expected gender norms are vulnerable to harassment based on this gender dissonance and their perceived sexual orientation. The findings of our research support such an argument, especially for males.

In the previous chapter, we provided examples where male participants experienced HTP bullying for lacking athletic prowess and wearing pink. In contrast, females, or those perceived as female, were picked on for wearing "masculine" clothing such as plaid shirts and for aggressiveness or fighting. Asked who was most often the target of homophobic or transphobic bullying, Ethan replied that people who were stereotypically gay or lesbian, "like really butch or really femme or whatever," were often singled out (Ethan, gay, male). From these participants' perspectives, many queer youth who are bullied dress, act or appear in ways that disrupt the sex-gender association (see also Bochenek and Widney 2001; Meyer 2007a; Walton 2006).

Walton (2006, i) identifies bullying as a technique of discipline and normalization that reinforces "normative gender expectations." Similarly, Meyer (2007a, 2) ties HTP bullying to "the public performance and norm-setting of heterosexual gender roles." She cites researchers with the Human Rights Watch who argue that HTP harassment often results from demands for strict adherence to norms for males or females (Bochenek and Widney 2001).

Traditionally, harassment for gender nonconformity has been classified as homophobia. Given the importance of gender expression in these incidents, however, we believe the focus should be not only on sexual orientation, but on gender variance as well (see Meyer 2006; Renold 2002; Walton 2006). In our research, gender expression may play an even more important role than one's sexual orientation in HTP victimization. Even students who do not identify as LGBTTQ can be bullied if their behaviour violates mainstream gender norms:

> A friend of mine... is not gay, but I guess is really assertive and athletic.... Some girl started a rumour that she and I were dating. (Sam, queer/gay, queer)

The same participant spoke about a girl who did openly identify as queer and presented some characteristics typically associated with femininity. This person, apparently, was not picked on:

> I was actually speaking to a friend of mine, who I knew to be queer at the time... but she was never really open about it and nobody ever really cared, because she's shy and not... out there. (Sam, queer/gay, queer)

In some cases, then, HTP harassment is sparked more by gender expression than by whether or not a young person identifies as queer (Nayak and Kehily 1996). Queer youth may receive opposite reactions to similar patterns of behaviour depending on their perceived gender. Earlier, Haley recalled an incident in which she stood up to a student threatening a classmate. She asserted herself and her sexuality, saying "You gonna call someone gay? Call me, I am! You gonna hit me? Do it now!" (Haley, lesbian/queer, female). Apparently, her offer was accepted and the male did punch her. Yet, as we also saw earlier, Nadeem (gay, male) found that standing up to others actually minimized the bullying he encountered. He said that showing self-confidence and holding his ground decreased the amount of HTP bullying he experienced.

We could argue that males who "fight back" may be less vulnerable to HTP harassment than assertive females because such actions by men fit well with the dominant form of masculinity. Females who stand up for themselves, on the other hand, may be more vulnerable than males to HTP harassment because assertiveness is discouraged in traditional notions of femininity. These hypotheses suggest that understandings of homophobic bullying cannot be limited to discussions of sexual identity. Gender expressions should thus be acknowledged as significant factors in both homophobic and transphobic bullying. Accordingly, it may be beneficial for those wanting to address HTP to not only reflect on how we encourage adherence to traditional gender norms but to reconceptualize how we think about gender in the first place.

A striking finding of our research was the "double standard" when it came to same-sex attraction. For the most part, social scientists tend to accept that female sexuality is more strictly regulated when compared with males. However, some participants said that this was not the case for gay or bisexual males. Phoenix explained:

> I did know a couple of guys in high school who were dating at the time when I was there and I definitely learned that... there's kind of a double standard between females and males when it comes to... acceptance of gay relationships.... Gay men seem to threaten people more for some reason. I think that's still true; a lesbian couple walking down the street holding hands would be less likely to be harassed than a gay male couple. (queer, androgynous)

Such observations match those of Varjas and her colleagues (2007). They reported that several participants in their study thought that high-school males received more negative reactions for engaging in same-sex relationships than did females. In addition, researchers with GLSEN found that students are more likely to hear remarks about not being "masculine" enough than not acting "feminine" enough (Kosciw et al. 2008, 16). Perhaps traditional ideas about masculinity are presupposed on heterosexuality (Pascoe 2007) in our culture more so than femininity (Meyer 2007b). Regardless, it is clear that gender and gender expression of the person targeted (as well as the harasser) figures into decisions to engage in HTP bullying and should be considered in future research on this topic.

Lack of Information about Queer People

The second theme in participants' discussions about the causes of HTP in schools is lack of information about queer people and issues affecting them. All of the young people we interviewed believed that silence about queer people and the issues affecting them fuelled homophobia and transphobia, which in turn further silences queer youth. They discussed the role of curriculum, a lack of role models, failure to intervene in HTP bullying, teacher training, religiosity and social conservatism, as well as larger social structures (i.e., law or health systems) in creating an environment ripe for HTP harassment.

High schools are commonly regarded as public spaces in which classroom discussions of private matters, including sexual or gender identity, should be formally off-limits (Loutzenheiser and MacIntosh 2004). Elaborating on this public-private distinction, some parents, students and members of the general public argue against inclusion of queer people in the curriculum, claiming that such discussions would undermine the values they teach at home. Many educational institutions have tried to avoid outcries of this nature by not acknowledging the existence of sexual minorities. The downside of this approach is that excluding entire segments of the population infringes upon others' values and beliefs as well. Researchers as far away as India have noted the silencing of sexuality in educational institutions (Tarun 2007, 128).

Some adults believe that discussing homosexuality in school will encourage children to experiment sexually, whereas silence or erasure will discourage homosexual behaviour (Blumenfeld and Raymond 1993). There is no evidence, however, that discussing sexuality and acknowledging various sexual identities encourages youth to "change" their sexual identity (Blumenfeld and Raymond 1993). Any perceived increase in the number of youth who identify themselves as queer is a result of feeling comfortable enough to assert their identity. Similarly, when homosexuality and transgenderism are cloaked in secrecy there may appear to be fewer young people who are LGBTTQ, but this perception is a consequence of an environment where youth feel unsafe to outwardly identify as queer.

Our participants held that educators, especially in rural and socially conservative schools, were hesitant to discuss issues affecting queer people. As one participant said:

> There's a complete absence of queer people in social studies.... That would be a start. Like even saying that you guys are a part of history too, right? (Ethan, gay, male)

The young people suggested changes to the curriculum to raise the visibility of queer people and awareness of issues affecting them. Corey talked about the potential of the Corren agreement in British Columbia ,which has led to the creation of an optional Grade 12 class on social justice issues, including homophobia (see Chapter One):

> It would be really great if [the Social Justice 12 class] went through.... Just to have that in the class, in the schools and then just to know those ideas are there, whether you take them or not, it's a pretty powerful force I think... to counter that kind of homophobia.... And to be honest, I don't actually ever see [queer issues] being integrated into the... required curriculum... but if there was an optional course, like the Corren agreement, that would really help. That is one way to get it in there. Because they can't say they're going to outlaw it if it's an optional course, right? (gay, male)

Others complimented teachers who included queer people in their lessons:

> [One teacher] just happened to mention that a guy in there was queer, like one of the guys who had made something.... I don't remember which

one it was, but it was just kind of random, came out of nowhere, but then she just kept going, and... it made it so natural. (Jamie, queer/gay, *)

Phoenix: I was in sex ed class... we got a sheet and the sheet had definitions of different words.... I still remember them, they were homosexual, bisexual and transgendered.... And it was not an atmosphere where you were supposed to be making fun of it, or cracking jokes, it was like you're learning something, just like you would learn anything else in this class. And that was also a really positive experience.... I remember seeing that list and it was like a light bulb over my head. It was like, "Ding!" I fit somewhere! Right on that sheet!
RH: That's good, then! So, inclusion in the curriculum I guess, especially during sex ed?
Phoenix: Yeah, I think [inclusion in the curriculum]... that's key. (queer, androgynous)

Participants cautioned that piecemeal efforts to raise awareness about HTP in schools were ineffective and advocated a more comprehensive approach to representing and supporting queer people in high school. Asked how they thought schools could be a better place for queer youth, participants in one group said:

Heather: They're just trying to do like the usual slap on the wrist or get the guest speaker, what not, and just hopefully that gets through their head, you know. Same thing with drunk driving, or drug abuse or whatever.
Trevor: The token guest speaker that everyone's going to laugh about the second they walk out of the assembly. (gay, male)
Heather: Yeah. So I just think that they just need to figure out a new approach for how to handle it. Because I know in CAPP (Career and Personal Planning), or whatever they call it now, they did a section of like safe sex, drug abuse... all that kind of crap. And then they did a thing on homosexuality, but it was like *one class*. You know, and you get to watch some movie from 1987 talking about "Are you gay?" (*, female)

In addition to a curriculum that includes queer people, participants thought it would be beneficial to have queer teachers as role models in the schools.

Many people in our study knew a school staff member who was lesbian, gay or bisexual but who was not open about it. Although they acknowledged that sexual orientation and gender identity might be private matters, participants said it was especially unlikely that a student could be "out" as LGBTTQ in an environment where teachers were not. Asked what they thought would help make schools safer for queer youth, participants answered:

> I think that it would be beneficial to have more queer and queer-ally role models. I think this would help normalize "queer" by showing people that "No, this is not a perversion. There are some very cool and even boring people who are queer and trans." (Sam, queer/gay, queer)

> Not being afraid to talk about it.... I had this one teacher, I knew she was gay, I knew that for a fact, and I tried bringing it up, like [in private] kind of thing and I know that it's their own privacy and stuff like that, and I totally respect her for not saying anything, but you still just want to tell someone, hey, I have something in common with you. And, just to make that connection, you know, and have them not be afraid of that. (Jamie, queer/gay, *)

Knowing a queer individual can foster positive attitudes about LGBTTQ people. Providing a space where potential role models feel safe to be "out" could reduce stigma and negative stereotypes about queer people and increase a sense of belonging for LGBTTQ youth (Burn 2000; Darwich 2008). Regardless of their sexual orientation or gender identity, school staff can help queer youth in their high schools by intervening appropriately when HTP incidents occur.

According to participants, teachers rarely seemed to recognize the damage caused by homophobic and transphobic actions. This sentiment is not isolated to B.C. Fully 52 percent of students in one Saskatchewan sample said that teachers rarely address HTP language (Cochrane and Morrison 2008). In the most recent GLSEN survey documenting experiences of queer students in the U.S., almost 31 percent of students report that school staff never intervene upon hearing homophobic remarks and 43 percent said the same about transphobic comments (Kosciw et al. 2008). Participants echoed these findings:

> They'd say "Oh, I'm going to do something about it."... Occasionally they'd even just tell us to tell them to... fuck off or whatever, but that's not going to help. That's just going to make it worse. (Trystan, gay, male)

> And that was I think the clearest and easiest way to get at someone was to call someone a fag or something like that. Because it was almost accepted. Teachers wouldn't do anything about it. It was the bullying that was acceptable... that you could get away with. (Corey, gay, male)

Twenty years ago, a task force investigating bias-related violence in New York State schools made the same observation. In that study, students actually "added a gratuitous vicious comment about gay people [to the survey], and appeared to perceive them as legitimate targets of hatred who can be openly attacked" (Radowsky and Siegel 1997, speaking of the State of New York Governor's Task Force on Bias-Related Violence 1988).

For the most part, participants did not consider that teachers were malicious if they failed to intervene. Staff were apparently unaware of how harmful HTP can be or unsure of how to deal with it when it surfaced. Other researchers identify a "teacher's lack of knowledge and... feelings of ineffectiveness when addressing highly charged issues" as factors limiting intervention (Birden 2005, 3). In our study, Phoenix condemned some of the educators for "turning a blind eye":

> They choose to turn a blind eye to it which just encourages the same behaviour to happen again and again.... I don't know, I just think it's so funny... if one kid called another kid nigger in school, you can pretty much be guaranteed that that kid would be in trouble.... They're choosing not to see it or they're choosing not to deal with it. Like, "Whatever! I'm going to go hang out in my teachers' lounge and drink my coffee and hide in here." (queer, androgynous)

Soon after, Phoenix surmised that teachers may not understand the impact of HTP language on queer youth:

> I think they're aware of it, but they just don't understand the weight behind it. I think they don't understand how much it can negatively impact someone's life in the long term... especially if they're not gay. (queer, androgynous)

At least two participants argued that when teachers intervene they need to do so in specific ways. Trevor thought that reactions should be quick and consistent:

> I find it's better, when [bullies] tend to act out and right away someone says that's wrong. Like the teachers that stand up... [the bullies] know that they can't tolerate it in the class so nobody's going to say anything because they don't want to get kicked out for something stupid, right? Or they'll still get kicked out anyways, they just don't care. But at least they're gone. (gay, male)

Another argued that teachers need to address the language being used. Failing to do so, Sam believed, contributes to the perception that terms such as "gay" and "queer" are bad words.

> The administration and teachers would rarely admonish people for calling others "fag," and if they did they would react the same way as if one was calling someone an asshole, the implication was that these were bad words. Fag, gay, homo, lesbian, transsexual, etc.... do not have to be bad words. It would be nice if teachers and students, when intervening in homophobic and/or transphobic bullying, could essentially get across "Your comments were obviously mean-spirited and when your words have harmful motives they are unacceptable" instead of "Don't say 'fag.' It is a bad word." (queer/gay, queer)

Haley said that teachers should be aware of their own behaviours before challenging those of youth. Elaborating on these thoughts, Haley said:

> Kids won't respect [others]. Because teachers will never respect them.... Pretty much every teacher talks down to every student. Kids aren't going to listen to that. They're going to rebel!... It's the whole adult-child syndrome. (lesbian/queer, female)

Alice Miller's (1990) work supports Haley's arguments. She describes the power relationships of teachers over students as "poisonous pedagogies" that breed a culture of violence. To ease bullying among students, Haley suggests that teachers' bullying of students must stop first.

Some participants gratefully acknowledged teachers who took a stand when students used HTP language. In one discussion group, participants who attended the same high school praised an outspoken, supportive teacher:

> Nadeem: My [History] teacher, she was amazing!... She had big posters on the front of her door that were like, "That's so gay" with a big X through it. And she was like, you don't call anyone "faggot" or anything in this classroom or you get out. (gay, male)
> Lukas: So many people got kicked out of her classroom for that. (bisexual, male)
> Nadeem: She was the best for that kind of stuff....
> Lukas: She would send you home! It would just be, like leave!
> Heather: Zero tolerance. Zero tolerance. (*, female)
> Lukas: There was zero tolerance for that kind of stuff.

There was one, I don't know if he was out... but, he was... a dancer and he danced quite a bit at shows and stuff and people would actually boo him while he was on stage.... And one teacher was really supportive of him... he tried to stop it.... He'd get right into the seats and shush people and just be like, "Be quiet" and "Don't do that." (Corey, gay, male)

At my school, teachers were really good about it. My... teacher, I'm not sure what [the student's] comment was, something about gay lifestyle... and then [the teacher] said, "Well, would you choose to be persecuted?" Or... "Why would you choose a harder life?" I thought that was pretty good. (Ethan, gay, male)

We were learning parts of the volcano and the teacher was explaining all the parts and... one part of it was a dyke. [Jamie giggles] Yeah, that's what it was like... and my teacher [said], "I don't want to hear anything from you guys if you have problems with it. I don't want to hear it!" There was just like silence through the whole classroom. (Xin, gay, gay)

These former students were clearly appreciative of teacher interventions. Unfortunately, because efforts to address homophobic and transphobic language were not school-wide, participants thought that HTP persisted, usually out of the earshot of those teachers who would intervene.

Participants believed that intervention efforts must be comprehensive. They appreciated the efforts of one or two supportive teachers who created a safe classroom but felt that the school climate could not change without the involvement of more staff. On the other hand, some questioned whether teachers should be responsible for intervening in and preventing HTP bullying. In one group, participants questioned whether teachers should be responsible for handling any kind of harassment and said that counsellors needed to take a more active role to raise awareness about homophobia and transphobia in high schools. Nadeem insisted:

It may sound crude, but [the teacher's] job is not to rescue little Johnny who just got picked on because he got called a faggot. That's what counsellors are for, that's what student safety administrators are for.... Those people should be enhanced... it shouldn't be laid on the teachers so much. (gay, male)

In support of Nadeem's take, Meyer (2007b) found that, when she asked six Canadian teachers why they did not intervene in HTP bullying, the most common theme in their responses related to time constraints to meet curriculum requirements. In leading efforts to educate their school community about HTP violence, counsellors may be able to provide enough base knowledge so that teachers could intervene in their classrooms without having to plan an entire lesson around the "teachable moment." In our study, participants believed that counsellors need to be more approachable and open to talking to queer youth. Explaining why he did not report the harassment he experienced in high school to school counsellors, Xander said:

> They need to be more approachable. There's that whole stigma! I mean, when everyone was coming up and asking me [if he was gay], I didn't feel like I could go to the counsellors. I didn't feel like I could just go into the office and be like, "They keep asking me this, and I don't know why." I never felt like I could go in and ask that sort of question. (gay/homosexual, male)

Heather added:

> I don't think... the friendly approach for help is there. Like, you know there are counsellors and you know they can help you, everyone always gets that typical thought in their head, like they're just going to sit there and listen and not tell you anything productive.... They're not doing a good job of saying, you know, "Hey if you need a shoulder." (*, female)

Demetrius believed his rapport with a school counsellor illustrated their positive impact on queer youth in high schools:

> I used to have a school counsellor, well, she didn't know anything about... situations of gay bullying, right? But even though I was out of school... I'd still... go to her office, and even though I wasn't part of the school anymore, she'd sit down and talk to me about situations I'm in. If there were more counsellors like that, I swear, every school would be a little bit better. Like, you don't have to deal with the bullies, but if you can at least help the student get it off their chest, or talk to them about it, you know, give them some sort of support, I think, things would be a lot better in schools. I don't know any other counsellor that was that supportive. (gay, male)

Like these youth, Rutter (2007) and Smith (1998) recommend that counsellors should actively support queer youth in schools.

Other participants urged students to speak up and challenge the homophobia and transphobia that exists in schools. For example, when asked why he thought HTP persists in high school, Trevor thought that students themselves should take the harassment more seriously and recognize the potential impact of their words:

> I think that a lot of people think that homophobia is a joke. It's like, it's okay, it's just a joke among their friends.... They joke about it too much, and they don't realize how serious it really is.... It's just the same as being racist!... and they don't seem to make... the connection there. And I think that's the problem.... Like if someone was to walk around the halls and start calling you nigger... everybody in the hall would probably smash them and throw them into a locker. But someone calls you a faggot, and nobody says anything. (gay, male)

Likewise, Nadeem believed that it was partly his (and other students') responsibility to do something about the HTP in his high school:

> I say okay, well, if my school's not gay-friendly, I'm going to make it gay-friendly. And I'm going to do everything I can, in my power, to get there. And so, I took on a bit of the onus in saying "Okay, if I just sit here and complain and don't do anything, that's what's going to happen, right?" I went to my counsellors and I went to my school and said, "Have you guys heard of [gay youth group], have you guys heard of all these places?" And they were like, "No, no, no," and I said, "Okay, here's the phone numbers, here's the addresses, call them, get information, and put that information out in the lobby for LGBT, transgender, whatever, to come and look at it." *Because otherwise it's not going to get done.* So I found that road really was productive... no one's going to do it for you. You have to do things for yourself. No one's going to say, "I'll go hunt down the bullies and find them for you." Like no one's going to do that. You have to be productive for yourself... it does take confidence, it does take guts, but, at least in my experience, it worked. (gay, male; emphasis added)

Researchers at Human Rights Watch (Bochenek and Widney 2001) and Kenway and Fitzclarence (1997) suggest that students can be agents of change. Young people should demand and develop means of addressing the harassment they face. In Kenway and Fitzclarence's (1997, 124) opinion, students should be treated as "agents rather than passive recipients of anti-violence reform." While GSAs are a popular way to provide a space for organizing against homophobia and transphobia in schools, some participants did not think this was the best option.

Contrary to some reports (Goodenow, Szalacha and Westheimer 2006; Radkowsky and Seigel 1997), not all participants were quick to relate the positive impact of Gay-Straight Alliances in their schools. Sam referred to a GSA during our interview session; when I asked whether it benefited them, they answered that ghettoization was sometimes the result:

> For whatever reason, I was the one who ended up being... stuck with it, you know I didn't perceive myself being stuck with it, but it was like after a while... the teacher sponsor of the GSA just kept on coming to me. And it was unfortunate because I'm not a very political person. And I was having a lot of personal problems at the time. (Sam, queer/gay, queer)

Another participant described his GSA as "horrible" and "stupid":

> It was just lots of things that were wrong with it. The first day they were like, "Okay, well introduce yourself and tell us your orientation" and that. I mean that's so... so... wrong! And then we all went around in a circle and I wasn't ready yet so I lied or whatever. But it was like, for someone who's questioning... [implying that it made it more difficult]... and they would even say, "Oh, you can trust everyone here," but really, can you? (Ethan, gay, male)

As discussed earlier in this chapter, sometimes queer youth abuse alcohol and drugs as a way to deal with the homophobia and transphobia they experience. Given this, Sam pointed out, GSAs and other queer youth groups may not be a positive influence. Talking about a queer person who became increasingly isolated from family and friends in high school and who relied more on a queer youth group for support, Sam said:

> She increasingly depended on people at [the queer youth group] to give her a place to crash if she didn't feel like she could go home. Unlike her high-school friends, many of these people who she started hanging out with were over nineteen and could get into clubs and bars and buy alcohol. They were self-supporting and did not depend on their parents in large part for money, and the jobs they held, if they even held jobs, were more flexible than high school which allowed them the ability to party a lot. They started bringing her to house parties. They introduced her to drugs stronger than marijuana by passing joints around that were laced with harder drugs like heroin and not informing her of this until afterwards.... She [became] addicted to crystal meth and dealing ecstasy. It was not

until a year later when she hit her rock bottom that she quit drugs entirely. (queer/gay, queer)

Despite evidence that queer youth may use alcohol and drugs as a means to cope with HTP they experience, most researchers applaud the benefits of GSAs without critically examining how substance abuse and queer youth groups intersect.

Another participant thought that high-school students were at a tough age to tackle such serious issues as HTP:

It's pretty rough, you know you have like Grade 8 kids who are immature.... I guess it's still when everyone's at that age where people are still not really sure of themselves. (Ethan, gay, male)

As part of this group discussion, another participant suggested that GSAs would benefit queer youth more if political issues were downplayed and social activities were emphasized.

Having more of a social setting, I think would get more students out, and then, of those students, only a portion of them would be activists, which is cool, but I think it's almost too much to ask of them.... If anyone had told me in high school, "Come to this meeting," I would have been like, "Um, no, I'm going to go hang out with my friends."... Like, let's have fun! Instead of "Today we're going to talk about issues, how's everybody doing today?", 'cause that just gets boring, I find. So having someone be like, "Let's go play hockey with all of us and then randomly get a table somewhere," like that kind of thing. (Jamie, queer/gay, *)

Some participants found that GSAs were worthwhile but there was considerable room for improvement. Asked how his GSA could have been better, Xin responded:

We only had... a regular three or four people every meeting, you know, and that was kind of sad.... We only had meetings at lunch time so I guess maybe we should have had it after school or something.... I guess that the one thing is that we should have had people actually in the hallways being like you should come to the GSA! Rather than on speaker phone, because, first of all, it's really tough, classrooms are pretty noisy and it's hard to talk over it... it doesn't address one-on-one, so it still makes you feel like you're still part of the whole, like lost in the crowd kind of feeling.

> Whereas if you talk to people one-on-one maybe you can get a better sense of who they are. (gay, gay)

Others shared some suggestions for improvement. Ethan talked about a particular initiative:

> They put on a poster campaign... [with] pictures of people and details about their bashing. So that was a good event, because people I saw stopped and I just saw how people reacted and were outraged. That was a good event. (gay, male)

Overall, participants stressed raising visibility of queer people in high schools (both students and staff) as well as increasing awareness about how seemingly innocuous homophobic and transphobic sentiments, language and behaviours can harm them. One way to raise awareness about HTP would to include the topic in teacher training. Most participants attributed teachers' and counsellors' ignorance or discomfort when it came to addressing HTP harassment to a lack of training or resources. They stressed the importance of teacher training about issues that affect LGBTTQ youth, either once they are hired or through professional development.

> If teachers were given... more training of accepting diversity in the classrooms, I think that would be really helpful. Like stopping that kind of homophobia when it happens in the classroom or even in the hallways, just taking a more proactive stance on it. (Corey, gay, male)

> Phoenix: If that was actually a part of teacher training and administrator training. If that was something that they learned in school or learned in the training process, or in a workshop, or something, you know. Like, this exists, we need to address it, and here's how you do it, and here's what's going on.
> RH: Do you think that's something that would have to be mandatory?
> Phoenix: I think that should be a mandatory part of teacher training. Like, not just homophobia, homophobia being one component of it, but homophobia, racism, classism, whatever. (queer, androgynous)

Participants believed that students, teachers and counsellors were not educated about homosexuality or gender variance and that, often, HTP stemmed from such ignorance. Other researchers have attributed teachers' failure to intervene in HTP bullying to feelings that administrators would not back their decision to do so and a lack of resources to deal with homophobia and transphobia (Meyer 2007b). In interviews with six Canadian teachers,

Meyer (2007b) found that those who had some training regarding homophobia and transphobia were more likely to intervene when they encountered such bullying. Decisions to intervene also hinged on the culture of the larger community in which the school was located, including the perceived level of social conservatism.

Although geographical location, social conservatism and religiousness are not always related, they were mentioned as a triad by several participants. Phoenix seemed to associate urban locations with acceptance, or at least awareness of issues affecting queer people:

> I think part of it is definitely geographical location. I went to... a school that's located... [in] Vancouver.... It's kind of in an area that's... becoming trendy and it's a little bit off beat already, so it's kind of alternative.... So I think that helped a lot and I think that it helped a lot to have teachers who came from that, also urban background. And had been dealing with, I mean, gay issues in the newspaper or around in the community. (queer, androgynous)

Nadeem also made reference to geographical locales:

> We're really lucky because we live in a great city that allows you to be really gay, like if you go to Vancouver, and open. You know. We're really lucky. But if you go to Abbotsford, maybe not so much. So... that's where I see it from too. You know, where I live. That's a huge part of it.... You couldn't be doing this in like Rwanda, for instance, where you get stoned to death if you're gay. Or you get killed in Iran if you're gay. (gay, male)

Other participants identified lack of awareness and social conservatism as factors contributing to HTP:

> I think there's a lot of positive things that happen, in like Vancouver and other more liberal places, but I think where things really need to be concentrated are places like [name of smaller city], [it's] not a small town but it's a really conservative town and... it could change so many people's lives, just by dealing with a city like that.
>
> I think that a lot of people just didn't know any better.... They weren't exposed to anything like that. They grew up in conservative households. (Corey, gay, male)

One participant believed people in her town were influenced by beliefs advanced by local religious leaders. Here she seems to associate church attendance with conservative beliefs. Asked if she agreed with Phoenix's assertion above that geographical location played a part in HTP harassment in high schools, Haley replied:

> Pretty much, yeah. Everyone goes to church [in the area she was in]. And if they don't go to church, their grandma goes to church.... I think it happens because of the parents. The parents don't accept [being gay], they take that down to you, put it down onto you, so you're not going to accept it, you're not going to understand it, you're going to be scared and you're going to take it out [on other people]. If your parents go to church, you're more likely to go to church. (lesbian/queer, female)

Haley reinforces what Radkowsky and Siegel (1997, 193) observed over a decade ago when they said that "the negative stance of most major organized religions toward homosexuality has greatly contributed to anti-gay bias in our society." Yet we acknowledge, as Karslake (2007) illustrates in his movie, *For the Bible Tells Me So*, that some religious people are supportive of queer people. Aside from some faith communities, participants believed that lessons about homosexuality and gender variance in other social and cultural institutions seeped into schools, including messages from the law and media.

A few participants thought that schools worsened the silencing of or negative messages about HTP people. Nadeem spoke of the historical maltreatment of LGBTTQ people by the state through law. Echoing his sentiment, Radkowsky and Siegel (1997, 193) conclude that, with the codification of homophobia and transphobia into religious teachings, legislation and formal policies, "anti-gay [and trans] bias is an intrinsic part of the socialization process for all youth."

Another participant (Nadeem, gay, male) implicated the media for portraying heterosexuality as the norm, a factor that he saw as increasingly influential given time invested in watching television or navigating the Internet. Ethan agreed that the media often fails to portray homosexuality and gender variance:

> When we were first getting started with the GSA we passed around this survey.... I remember reading one of them, [they] said it's just something that... isn't very common, isn't as portrayed as much [in the media] and that's why people are scared of it, they're scared of... difference... and they just see it as something that's completely foreign. (gay, male)

Not only do the media convey their own biases, they also report on those of others. In his research on queer youth and suicide, Kitts (2005, 625) poignantly notes that a young person does not need to be directly victimized to be affected by discrimination against gays.

> Matthew Shephard, a University of Wyoming student, was brutally murdered in 1998 because he was gay. What impact did this devastating event have on young individuals who were beginning to realize that they too were gay and living in the same society in which the murder was praised? What messages are protestors and politicians, including our President, who are against gay marriage sending to gay adolescents? How does living in a society where people can be rejected, disapproved of, or hated for their sexuality affect a gay adolescent's self-esteem or identity development?

Kitts's words can be applied to our current-day Canadian climate. In 2001, Aaron Webster, a gay man, was bludgeoned to death in Vancouver, and as recently as 2009, twenty-seven-year-old Chris Skinner of Toronto was fatally beaten and his body run over with an SUV in an apparent gay bashing (Salerno 2009). Non-fatal attacks happen even in the most diverse of Canadian cities (Janoff 2005). On the political front, Prime Minister and Conservative Party Leader Stephen Harper and several Conservatives have failed to support measures aimed at extending the human rights or protection of LGBTTQ people. For example, upon his election in 2006, Prime Minister Harper and the majority Conservative government brought forth a proposal to overturn the law that made same-sex marriage legal in Canada ("Canada Upholds" 2006). A Conservative MP was demoted after supporting a gay pride event in 2009 ("Gay Pride Cash" 2009), and in 2010, the Minister of Immigration removed any mention of same-sex rights in a study guide for immigrants applying for Canadian citizenship (Beeby 2010). These messages from larger society have an impact, not only on queer youth, but on others who learn that LGBTTQ people do not deserve to be treated as respectable citizens of our nation, let alone in our schools.

Bullying As a Normal Part of Growing Up
Some participants viewed bullying, including HTP harassment, as an inevitable part of growing up. High school might be a time when homophobia and transphobia are prevalent because students are reaching sexual maturity and yet are still immature. When asked why HTP harassment happened in high school, Sam answered:

> I think that homophobic and transphobic bullying happened in my high school because that's when for a lot of people sexual feelings really start raging so there's a greater awareness of sexuality in general and it becomes important to define... "normal" sexual feelings.... Now that

> people are more aware of queer/trans issues and of the idea that sexual
> orientation is intrinsic maybe people feel as though they have more to
> prove. Maybe in order to reinforce the idea that they're heterosexual or
> avoid any ambiguity, bullying is a way of showing one's sexual orientation
> by asserting what one finds to be repugnant... by asserting what one is
> by asserting what one is not? (queer/gay, queer)

Herek (1992, 156) makes a similar assertion about the roots of prejudice against queer people: homophobia "helps people to define who they are by directing hostility toward gay people as a symbol of what they are not." Similarly, Pascoe (2007) and Kimmel (1994) regard homophobic behaviour as an assertion of heterosexual masculinity. Some participants discussed the role of sexual differentiation in HTP bullying in a slightly different context. Trevor wondered whether one youth's persistent harassment was a result of his latent homosexuality:

> He seemed to pay attention to me more than anybody else. I almost think
> he was gay... because he just seemed to, like, I don't know, I took off my shirt
> or something and like... he... made some weird stupid comment. (gay, male)

Other participants thought bullying was a result of insecurities that are sometimes a normal part of adolescence or teen years. Problems at home may heighten these insecurities:

> A lot of the people were in really tough situations... so I think they had a
> lot of problems at home.... Just about everyone I knew came from broken
> families or abusive families, their parents were drug dealers, there were
> quite a few [like that]. So, they had a lot of issues that I think they needed
> to deal with and they kind of dealt with it by putting other people down I
> think. (Corey, gay, male)

To counteract HTP messages at home and in the media, participants underlined the importance of positive representations of queer people in schools. They believed that students and staff should be educated about the potential impact of HTP language and behaviours in schools. One participant openly questioned the extent to which inclusion of LGBTTQ people in school curriculum would challenge lessons learned at home.

> I think they can put an influence on the kid's life, but the chances of chang-
> ing it are slim to none. Because when they get home it'll go back to how
> their parents are. (Haley, lesbian/queer, female)

Phoenix, the other participant in this small group, disagreed with Haley:

> I think that they can. I don't know... just kind of teach kids that it's okay to believe what you believe, but, you know, it's not okay to push it onto others. And, teach people, you know, respect! That's all it is, just respect. (queer, androgynous)

Phoenix and Haley were unsure of the extent to which HTP bullying could, or should, be challenged in high school. Instead, they believed that the most severe bullying should be addressed. Asked how we could address HTP in high schools, these participants said:

> Haley: You'll never be able to stop it.
> Phoenix: Yeah. You can't stop it. For sure.
> Haley: And for one thing, I would never want to stop it. Because it does help people grow. It just needs to be... lessened.
> Phoenix: Yeah, definitely! (queer, androgynous)
> Haley: It's really extreme. Back in the day, two guys got in a fight, [and afterward, they'd say], "Okay, let's go get a drink now!' Nowadays, it's not the same.
> RH: Why do you think it will never stop?
> Haley: Human nature. (lesbian/queer, female)

Following up on this exchange, Phoenix said they thought that bullying might be a normal part of growing up. They agreed with Haley that bullying could not be eradicated completely, but thought that it needed to be reduced:

> I do agree with that.... You could give everyone, all the students and all the teachers all the sensitivity and awareness training that you wanted and then you'd still have some kid walk up to another kid and go "Fuck you, fucking faggot!" and punch him in the face. It would still happen. It's just kids... it's just part of growth. But I just, I don't think that it should be at the level of intimidation that it's at recently. (Phoenix, queer, androgynous)

Most of us can probably agree with calls to address the most severe forms of bullying. The contention that other forms of harassment cannot, and perhaps should not, be addressed, however, is more controversial. The problem, we believe, with saying that we need to address the extremity of HTP bullying lies in the invisibility of subtle forms of HTP harassment. In these participants' experiences, physical violence is not the dominant form of HTP bullying; yet, this is where our focus remains. By proposing to tolerate subtle bullying, we contribute to the invisibility of the most frequent manifestations of homophobia and transphobia and exacerbate perceptions of harmlessness when they are visible. In addition, less visible forms of HTP create environments where physical manifestations may take place, undermining any effort to reduce those forms as well.

Rather than focusing on more extreme forms of harassment, we need to raise awareness about more frequent and subtle manifestations of HTP and the effects they have on queer youth. Working to address the underlying homophobic and transphobic sentiments and to debunk the stereotypes that fuel them would go a long way toward reducing subtle and extreme manifestations alike (Khayatt 1994). This assertion is the focus of the concluding chapter, in which major findings and themes are reviewed and discussed using the theoretical works of Foucault and Bourdieu.

Bourdieu and Foucault produced complex, demanding bodies of work. We make no claim to include a comprehensive, authoritative outline of the writings of these theorists. Instead, a few of their more developed concepts are presented to complement the empirical work of this book and to generate discussions about new ways of thinking about HTP bullying and how best to respond to it.

Chapter 4

A Gentle Violence?

> Knowledge can be emancipatory. The better we understand the external constraints on our thoughts and action, the more we will see through them and the less effective they will become. (Hoy 1999, 18)

As Hoy (1999) points out, knowledge can help us to become more aware of power relations and appreciate how they shape and are shaped by social norms. In this final chapter, the works of Michel Foucault and Pierre Bourdieu are used to clarify the most prevalent themes of this study on HTP in Canadian high schools. First, parallels are drawn between Foucault's (1977) discussion of shifts in techniques of discipline in the 1800s and forms of HTP bullying in high school. Bourdieu's (1991) concept of symbolic violence is useful to describe the more subtle forms of HTP that seem to characterize high schools today. Second, it is argued that high schools constitute a "surveillance society" (Foucault 1977) in which sexual orientation and gender identity, or the behaviours and mannerisms often associated with them, are closely scrutinized. The effects of such careful monitoring on what Bourdieu (1991) terms the "habitus" are detailed. Finally, this chapter highlights how participants' recommendations for change, and perhaps this research project in general, are in line with Bourdieu and Foucault's call for "desubjugation," challenging social hierarchies that are normally taken for granted.

Participants' recommendations are valuable as policy recommendations in their own right, but grounded in theory they are invaluable. As Winfree and Abadinsky (2003, 15) observe:

> Policies that are devoid of theoretical underpinnings… may have limited utility, as they may meet immediate needs if based on current research but be unable to meet the demands of a changing society.

Following Foucault and Bourdieu, we believe that even knowing which forms of HTP are most frequent and which are least likely to be addressed provides a starting place for change. Before applying some of the theories of Foucault and Bourdieu to HTP bullying, we provide a brief overview of their relevant work.

Michel Foucault and Pierre Bourdieu: A Brief Introduction

As our research progressed, themes of oppression, normalization and resistance emerged. These themes are also found in the works of Bourdieu and Foucault. We found Bourdieu and Foucault's concepts useful for exploring power relations in general and, more specifically, how power serves to both regulate and subvert expressions of gender and sexuality. In addition, the theorists' emphasis on researching power relations from a "bottom-up" perspective (Middleton 1998) made them especially compatible with our research design. For example, it was important to us that the young people, who typically do not hold much power in policy or political realms, be treated as experts on HTP bullying.

Using the works of Foucault and Bourdieu and relying on participants' conjectures, we meant to contribute to understandings about homophobic and transphobic harassment in high schools. One way to do this is to explore what exactly is happening in terms of types of bullying, but also to analyze the power relations at work. In this book we have examined the extent to which queer youth and other members of high schools consciously recognize the hierarchies that are being enforced. Also noted is whether the form that HTP harassment takes factors into such acknowledgements. Addressing these issues necessarily involves an exploration of power relations that work to perpetuate norms and hierarchies through social interactions, including those that are homophobic or transphobic. As such, an understanding of Foucault and Bourdieu's views on power and socialization is useful from the beginning.

Pierre Bourdieu (1939–2002) and Michel Foucault (1926–1984) were French philosophers whose works have remained influential since they became popular during the political movements of the 1960s and 1970s (Hoy 2004) (see <www.foucaltsociety.org> for more information about Foucault). Although neither scholar aligned himself with any specific theoretical camp, both can be classified as critical theorists and have been labelled as poststructuralist, neo-structuralist and postmodern thinkers (Hoy 2004; Swartz 1997). Other critical thinkers such as Friedrich Nietzsche and Maurice Merleau-Ponty were heavily influential in their thinking (Hoy 2004). The theorists focus on power, social relations and social structures, including institutions, but their thinking differs in various ways. For example, Bourdieu is more focused on "persistence and continuity" in power relations and social norms whereas Foucault highlights the "transience and discontinuity" of the same things (Hoy 1999, 4). Bourdieu emphasizes the stability of learned behaviours more so than Foucault, who seems to leave more room for agency and change (Hoy 1999). In other ways, the authors are aligned.

Bourdieu and Foucault encourage us to be aware of social hierarchies that many of us take for granted. They concentrate on how disparate power relations are often accepted by those who occupy less valued positions in society. For example, in discussing techniques of discipline implemented in the penal system during the 1800s, Foucault (1977, 303) urges researchers to ask: "How were people made to accept the power to punish, or quite simply, when punished, tolerate doing so?" Bourdieu focuses on "how stratified social systems of hierarchy and domination persist and reproduce intergenerationally without powerful resistance and without the conscious recognition of their members" (Swartz 1997, 6). He refers to this phenomenon, in which social classifications and hierarchies are so easily reproduced, as the "paradox of doxa" (Bourdieu 2001, 1).

Due to their focus on everyday interactions, Bourdieu and Foucault have been described as taking micro approaches to explain power relations. For example, in discussing his conception of power, Foucault (1980, 39) says:

> But in thinking of the mechanics of power, I am thinking rather of its capillary form of existence, the point where power reaches into the very grain of individuals, touches their bodies and inserts itself into their actions and attitudes, their discourses, learning processes and everyday lives.

Bourdieu also focuses on where power "inserts itself into" (Foucault 1980, 39) an individual's actions and attitudes, giving special attention to its effects on our dispositions and beliefs. As the theorists see it, power relations are a part of all social interactions, even though this is not often readily apparent.

According to Foucault and Bourdieu, social interactions inherently involve power relations and teach us dominant norms, or what Bourdieu terms "the cultural arbitrary." Norms govern our behaviour, including those related to sexuality and gender. When internalized, these norms are often perceived as natural inclinations. They are reproduced, however, consciously and unconsciously as we regulate the behaviour of others as well as ourselves. Our tendency to take these norms for granted may well legitimize power relations. Consequently, we sometimes overlook the social and historical conditions that have created them (Thomson in Bourdieu 1991, 5).

In relation to this research, Bourdieu and Foucault see norms relating to sexuality and gender as social constructs, a product of socialization rather than nature or natural proclivities. Homophobic and transphobic bullying, as forms of power and discipline, function as lessons (often referred to as the hidden curriculum), teaching us which behaviours and associated identities are valued and which are not. To avoid negative responses (or HTP harassment), youth learn to enact those behaviours and adopt those identities that are valued. As outlined earlier in this book, however, many queer youth choose silence, inaction or even death over engagement in gendered and sexually normative performances.

Far from being natural, then, our behaviours when it comes to sexuality and gender expression "are caught up in and moulded by the forms of power and inequality which are pervasive features of societies" (Thomson in Bourdieu 1991, 2). Homophobic and transphobic bullying, therefore, are not natural reactions to unnatural sexual inclinations or gender expressions, as sexual and gender norms are themselves social constructs that are taught and reinforced throughout the socialization process. As Bourdieu (2000, 152) says, "The body is in the social world... but the social world is in the body."

Bourdieu and Foucault see socialization, or the internalization of norms, as a diffuse process that cannot be attributed to one person or institution in particular. Both authors, however, identify educational institutions as key sites that impart social norms. As such, their works are very relevant to this research and help to ground the recommendations presented in this final chapter.

In the group discussions, participants offered a glimpse of what had been going on in their schools, sharing experiences of HTP bullying and how they had been personally affected, then and now. Recommendations made in this final section come from these young queer people who have experienced harassment and who wish to reduce homophobia and transphobia in high schools. In addition, we believe that the recommendations promote awareness about power relations and expand our thinking about gender identity or expression and sexual orientation. Foucault advocates raising awareness of the range of possibilities neglected under the status quo (Hoy 1999, 82). We hope that our recommendations will "shake up habitual ways of working and thinking" (Foucault 1996, 462) and open a space for reflection and dialogue about some of the taken-for-granted assumptions related to social norms and hierarchies in our society and schools. With this theoretical outlook on power and resistance in mind, we return to the topic of bullying of LGBTTQ students and emerging forms of resistance to such bullying.

From the "Spectacle" of Physical Violence to "Gentle Violence"

The first areas explored in this study were the forms, frequency and context of HTP bullying in B.C. high schools. We found that subtle forms of harassment (i.e., verbal harassment, exclusion, general heterosexism and genderism) are the most common forms of HTP participants experienced. Yet, some young people reported that physical harassment motivated by sexual orientation or gender identity persists in B.C. high schools. Foucault's (1997) discussion of discipline and punishment is useful in contextualizing this persistence.

In *Discipline and Punish* (1977), Foucault traces the shift in techniques of discipline in the eighteenth and nineteenth centuries. The eighteenth century featured corporal forms of discipline such as torture to make an example of the guilty. Foucault says that a small group of people (those in power) subjected others to inordinate amounts of pain and torture aimed at instilling fear in the population and acting as a general deterrent. In this era, and through the "spectacle," the unruly body was "the major target of penal repression" (Foucault 1977, 8). Similarly, we argue, the use of physical discipline in schools to promote gender conformity is characteristic of the "society of spectacle" in which punishment is designed to set an example and to induce adherence to bodily and behavioural norms.

Treating educational institutions as sites of discipline, Middleton (1998, 9) argues that "throughout the educational histories of Western countries, male and female bodies have been subjected in schools to normalizing practices which reinforce this opposition." In her analysis of school bullying, Middleton describes efforts to enforce gender norms directed at the body, in the form of corporal punishment, a technique used in many schools until the mid–twentieth century:

> Many (but not all) schools demanded that teachers administer corporal punishment in order to avoid being positioned as "weak" or "soft" by their colleagues and students. Authority was, at least in part, equated with physical stature and with strength, a quality deemed to be lacking in women and suspect in men with smaller bodies.... Corporal punishment can be read as complicit in the construction of embodied masculinity and embodied femininity. (Middleton 1998, 36)

Corporal punishment has been prohibited in Canada since 2004, at least at the hands of teachers. Yet, as participants pointed out, physical aggression persists, mostly among students.

Physical force can work to validate one's own hegemonic femininity or masculinity. With the decline of corporal punishment, this imperative may have transferred from school authorities to the student body. By failing to curtail students' efforts to monitor and regulate gender transgressions, it is possible that teachers and administrators tacitly grant permission for youth to perform the physical punishments they can no longer mete out. Along with the transfer of power to punish through physical means, the instruments of discipline shifted as well; what was once carried out through external tools (straps, rulers and canes) became an embodied practice with the use of fists, feet and other body parts. Yet, as Foucault argues about discipline in the nineteenth century, we argue here that there may have been a profound shift from spectacular and physical forms of harassment to more subtle yet effective manifestations of HTP.

In the nineteenth century, Foucault (1977) argues, there was a shift from the "spectacle" of physical violence to the "surveillance society." Foucault sees discipline operating so efficiently in modern society that he compares it to a "machine." He attributes this efficiency to a diffusion of, first, the power to discipline, and second, the people targeted. According to Foucault, discipline is no longer directed from one body to another, nor characterized by exorbitant amounts of force. On the contrary, modern techniques of discipline are used by, and targeted at, the entire social body. With everyone able to monitor everybody, discipline has become much more universal and yet much less noticeable. Modern forms of discipline, Foucault (1977) argues, serve a "generalized function," discouraging those who transgress social norms from doing so again at the same time as they deter others from wanting to do so in the first place. Of course, people find ways to push back and resist any form of discipline, and these forms of power are discussed later in this chapter.

Like Foucault, Bourdieu (1991) focuses on "invisible" forms of discipline and uses the term "symbolic power" to describe them. He defines symbolic power as "a power of constructing reality, and one which tends to establish a *gnoseological* order: the immediate meaning of the world (and in particular of the social world)" (Bourdieu 1991, 166; emphasis in original). We can see symbolic power at work in the social hierarchies that tend to value certain sexual identities and gender expressions over others. When one operates under the assumption that social hierarchies are natural (or misrecognizes that they are socially constructed) and imposes that view on others, a form of symbolic violence has taken place (Bourdieu 1990). Symbolic violence involves:

> [a] power of constituting the given through utterances, of making people see and believe, of confirming or transforming the vision of the world and thus the world itself. It is a power that can be exercised only if it is recognized, that is misrecognized as arbitrary. (Bourdieu, 1991, 170)

Symbolic violence is exercised when teachers or students frame heterosexuality as the only, or at least the normal, sexual orientation. This occurs, for example, through a curriculum that erases, or at least overlooks, queer people in its assumptions that students are heterosexual, and through HTP harassment itself. Gender expressions are also caught up in symbolic power relations: certain behaviours and appearances are valued over others, based on one's perceived biological sex. In relation to gender, educators exert symbolic violence when they impose their perceptions of gender norms. For example, a P.E. teacher may encourage a young man to engage in the "rough and tumble" sport of football rather than the graceful athleticism of gymnastics. Even subtle forms of HTP strengthen the perception that LGBTTQ identities and appearances, or the behaviours associated with them, are unnatural and unacceptable, constituting a form of symbolic violence. As Bourdieu (1991, 51) says,

The ways of looking, sitting, standing, keeping silent, or even of speaking ("reproachful looks" or "tones," "disapproving glances" and so on) are full of injunctions that are powerful and hard to resist precisely because they are silent and insidious, insistent and insinuating.

When experienced by queer people, Bourdieu (2001, 119) argues, symbolic violence "takes the form of a denial of public, visible existence." "Invisibilization," a neologism coined by Bourdieu, denies social and legal legitimacy and encourages stigmatization of those who attempt to make themselves visible (Bourdieu 2001, 119). In high schools, subtle or symbolic forms of violence lead to the harassment of youth who do not exhibit behaviours or appearances associated with valued identity categories (such as heterosexuality and gender conformity). This harassment, in turn, leads young queer people to hide or make themselves invisible. "Invisibilization" encourages people to deny, or overlook, the fact that there may be people (some LGBTTQ) who are offended or affected by homophobia and transphobia. This is especially true in high-school contexts where young people are present. Consequently, educational institutions, often perceived as apolitical fields, may be carrying out a form of symbolic violence (and condoning other forms of aggression) as they quietly reinforce dominant worldviews (Bourdieu and Passeron 1990).

Bourdieu and Passeron (1990, 4) say that symbolic violence "constitutes a form of violence precisely because it "generates the illusions that it is not violence." Speaking of this illusion, Bourdieu (2001, 1) describes symbolic violence as "a gentle violence, imperceptible and invisible even to its victims." Subtle, constant techniques of discipline are more effective and more likely legitimized precisely because they go unrecognized as forms of power. This "misrecognition," as Bourdieu often calls it, of subtle forms of homophobia and transphobia was evident in participants' narratives, especially in their struggles to define bullying.

Although physical harassment was not the most frequent form of bullying reported in this study, participants (as do most others) seemed to focus on addressing "extreme" forms of HTP over other subtle but more frequent manifestations. When recalling subtle forms of harassment that seem to flourish in heterosexist and gender-limiting school environments, most participants compared them to the physical harassment others sometimes face and downplayed their own experiences. Participants' belief that "it could have been worse" raises the question of when and why *any* level of homophobia or transphobia is acceptable.

We argue that more attention needs to be given to "gentle" forms of HTP violence; surely more extreme forms of homophobia and transphobia will flourish as long as more subtle manifestations persist. Participants discussed the role of teachers, teachers training, counsellors and students themselves in intervening and raising awareness about subtle HTP in B.C. high schools. The most resonant theme of all of these recommendations, however, was that someone needs to intervene.

Creating Docile Bodies

> There is no need for... physical violence... just a gaze. An inspecting gaze, a gaze which each individual under its weight will end by interiorising to the point that he is his own overseer, each individual thus exercising this surveillance over, and against, himself. In this "machine," no one is exempt from the gaze; everyone is at once the surveyor and the surveyed. (Foucault 1980, 155)

In our study, we were also interested in the impact of HTP on queer youth in high school. As socially constructed and valued identity categories, heterosexuality and gender conformity are promoted and enforced in high-school environments by students and teachers alike. As a result, students learn to behave in ways that allow them to "pass" by stifling cues often associated with queer identities. Bourdieu (1991, 52) would argue that queer youth "learn not only to act. The power of suggestion... instead of telling the child what he must do, tells him what he is, and this leads him to become durably what he has to be."

At a time when most young people are "learning how to socialize, young [queer] people are learning to conceal large areas of their lives from family and friends" (Hetrick and Martin 1984, 11). Participants' self-censorship in high school and in the years after graduation form part of what Foucault terms the "surveillance society," referred to above. Central to the surveillance society is the Panopticon, a prison design and penal device designed by Jeremy Bentham to increase surveillance. Foucault (1980, 147) describes the innovation as

> [a] perimeter building in the form of a ring. At the centre of this, a tower, pierced, by large windows opening on the inner face of the ring. The outer building is divided into cells each of which traverses the whole thickness of the building. These cells have two windows, one opening to the inside, facing the windows of the central tower, the other, outer one allowing daylight to pass through the whole cell. All that is then needed is to put an overseer in the tower and place in each of the cells a lunatic, a patient, a convict, a worker or a schoolboy.

Generalizing from the concept of the Panopticon, Foucault says an "inspecting gaze" characterizes modern society and current techniques of discipline, creating a panoptic society (1980, 155). In this "machine," we are each "the gaze," but we are also subject to it. Under this regime, we monitor and encourage behaviours congruent with social norms and stifle those that are not. Foucault (1980, 107) terms this new era the "society of normalization."

High school is a time when gender expression and sexuality are monitored and often judged. The association of adolescence with sexual maturity leads to hyper-surveillance of students by school staff and classmates, and even themselves. Student bodies are sexualized, with an increasing number of behaviours read as indicators of homo- or heterosexuality. Through HTP harassment, adherence to heterosexual gender norms becomes an imperative. Consequently, students subject themselves to the "inspecting gaze" just as much as they do their classmates (and their classmates, them), creating a "surveillance society" within educational institutions. Speaking of the surveillance society, Foucault (1977, 304) says:

> The judges of normality are present everywhere.... Each individual, wherever he may find himself, subjects to it his body, his gestures, his behaviour, his aptitudes, his achievements.

Certainly, such surveillance does not cease once youth leave the high-school environment. Bourdieu (1990) might argue that HTP affects participants in the long-term because of its impact on the "habitus." Experiences with heterosexism and genderism, along with HTP harassment, teach us enduring lessons through which "the whole social order imposes itself at the deepest level" of ourselves (Bourdieu 1990, 75). Once internalized, norms related to sexuality and gender and the corresponding behaviours expected of us become part of what Bourdieu terms the "habitus." The habitus, Bourdieu (1991) explains, can be seen as our second nature. We determine appropriate courses of action, or know "how to act and respond in the course of [our] daily lives" by comparing present experiences with the circumstances in which the habitus was developed (Bourdieu 1991, 13). Put into action, these (pre) dispositions are termed a "bodily hexis," "a durable way of standing, speaking, walking and thereby of feeling and thinking" (Bourdieu, 1990, 69–70). Our bodily hexis informs our behaviours, which are practised in a manner that is wholly unconscious, leading Bourdieu to view the habitus as "not so much a state of mind as a state of body" (Bourdieu 1991, 13).

According to Bourdieu, social interactions, including HTP harassment, tell us not only how to behave but also which identities are accepted and should be adopted and developed (Bourdieu 1991, 52). Whether they experience HTP directly or not, youth in high school may learn to suppress behaviours and avoid activities that are associated with devalued queer identities and that lead to harassment. Rather than merely stifling characteristics associated with LGBTTQ identities, some youth go to great lengths to prove that they are straight, or adopt a straight habitus. Because aggression is often associated with hegemonic (or dominant forms of) masculinity and heterosexuality, young males may engage in aggressive behaviours and activities, particularly HTP harassment, to avoid being targeted themselves.

Once internalized into our habitus, Bourdieu (1991) says, our thoughts and behaviours are almost automatic. Bourdieu (2001) asserts that internalization and adherence to norms relating to gender and sexuality is a largely unconscious process that does not easily lend itself to undoing. Heterosexist and gender-limiting environments, including some high schools in which queer people are not portrayed or discussed in a positive light, are contexts in which we learn that heterosexuality and gender conformity are the norm. The natural appearances of behaviours associated with hegemonic identities, such as male aggression, make them especially resistant to reflection and change. Consequently, the habitus becomes part of the taken-for-granted normative model that created it, strengthening and legitimizing power relations in society. Our failure to critically reflect on social norms ingrained in us contributes to sustained denigration of certain behaviours and the (queer) identities associated with them (Bourdieu 1991).

That participants in this study were able to discuss the ways they consciously monitored their own behaviours calls into question Bourdieu's contention about the unconscious nature and durability of the habitus. In another study, Nayak and Kehily (1996, 217) found that "acting straight" or conveying "heterosexual masculinity" was a constant performance for the youth they spoke with. These findings contest Bourdieu's belief that behaviours become so ingrained that they become second nature.

In focusing on the oppressive nature of socialization, Bourdieu does not seem to account for the critical thinking skills also encouraged through everyday interactions. Analytical thinking and reflexivity may be just as enduring as other traits Bourdieu identifies as part of the habitus. It makes sense that our past interactions and experiences influence our future behaviour, but we believe that Bourdieu downplays our ability to "think grey," that is, to recognize our world outside binary categories. Alternatively, in his concept of the docile body, Foucault leaves open the possibility of resistance.

Foucault (1977, 137) believes that modern forms of discipline (i.e., surveillance and other subtle forms of control) are effective at "obtaining holds upon [the body] at the level of the mechanism itself — movements, gestures, attitudes, rapidity; an infinitesimal power over the active body." Subtle, constant and unnoticeable forms of discipline produce what Foucault (1977, 138) calls "subjected and practised bodies, 'docile' bodies." A docile body,

Foucault (1977, 136) says, is one "that may be subjected, used, transformed and improved"; in other words, the docile body is open to discipline.

Applying these theoretical insights to our study, one could argue that exposure to HTP in high schools had the impact of creating "docile bodies." We can see evidence of this in the young people's adoption of cues that would encourage others in their high school to see them as straight (or distanced them from the abject "other," or queer identity). The characteristics they attempted to adopt, as well as those they stifled, do not indicate any sexual or gender identity in and of themselves; on the contrary, the young people in this study operated under assumptions and definitions imposed by peers in their school and other aspects of larger society

Foucault does not view the creation of the docile body as a result of top-down power relations, domination or of one body controlling the strings of another (we are thinking here, of course, of a marionette). Instead, Foucault imagines every body as powerful. The power of the docile body, however, has been coercively directed toward certain behaviours. Because each of us holds some degree of power, there is always potential for its reformulation and for resistance. In our study, several participants said negative experiences propelled them to make more positive changes in their high school or at least in their peer group.

According to Foucault and Bourdieu, subtle forms of discipline play an important role in normalization. Encouraging critical reflection about the subtle ways we are induced to adhere to norms, however, creates an opportunity for youth to challenge inherent social hierarchies. The youth in this sample were able to reflect on and call into question the norms that lead to the HTP they experienced. Providing a venue for other young people to engage in critical thinking may help to raise awareness about, and ultimately create resistance to, HTP in high schools.

Pushing Back against Oppression in School

As noted in the introduction, there is a tendency for researchers to focus on oppressive practices and to downplay the agency of participants (Darwich 2008; Fox 2004; Savin-Williams 1990). Theorists have urged researchers to acknowledge how people resist oppression. This book attempts to do so by highlighting the way participants pushed back against HTP in their high schools.

Sex and sexuality are central concerns in our society. The paradox in such a fascination is the proliferation of discourses (words, thought, discussion, writing and so on) around sexuality and an increasing desire to engage in them. Discourse is a powerful tool of oppression but also for resistance, depending on the strategy used and the person who is speaking. In this sense, the same words can have very different meanings. Foucault (1990, 101) explains:

> Discourse can be both an instrument and an effect of power, but also a hindrance, a stumbling-block, a point of resistance and a starting point for an opposing strategy.... It reinforces [power], but also undermines and exposes it, renders it fragile and makes it possible to thwart it.

Foucault argues that the increasing use of labels to create categories (e.g., in the medical or psychological fields) can sometimes lead to denigration; however, it also opens a space for a "reverse discourse." Although Foucault (1990, 101) speaks in terms of medical categories, in general, reverse discourses make it possible for queer identities to speak on "[their] own behalf,... demand that [their] legitimacy or 'naturality' be acknowledged, often in the same vocabulary, using the same categories by which [they] were... disqualified."

In Chapters Two and Three, participants expressed the belief that queer people were rarely discussed in their high schools. When LGBTTQ people were referenced, it was often in a negative light. For example, although participants did not agree on the impact of such words, most of them heard phrases such as "you're a fag" quite frequently in their high schools. According to participants, staff and students rarely intervened upon hearing such insults. One participant said that teachers who *did* intervene framed words associated with queer identities as "bad words." Several authors in the field (Meyer 2006, 2007b; Pascoe 2007; Walton 2006), however, have suggested that situations where LGBTTQ people are denigrated can be seen as teachable moments. These opportunities provide a space to challenge negative perceptions and misconceptions about queer people. Presenting students with a reverse discourse to negative perceptions of homosexuality and gender variance enables them to engage with it and to use it themselves. In this study some participants generated reverse discourses of their own.

We have attempted to present ways participants resist oppressive power relations, including their creation and use of reverse discourses. Participants shared various ways they pushed back against the HTP harassment they encountered through humour and physical violence, and by channelling the oppressive power into more constructive endeavours. In fact, three participants described their high-school experiences as generally positive, mostly because they found support from classmates and staff, but also because they worked to create a safe environment for themselves. Some participants resisted "victim" labels by volunteering for this study with the express intention of discussing positive experiences and how HTP helped them to grow. Positive experiences are especially useful in exploring their possible replication and what changes could be made so that queer youth in high schools feel safe.

Participants who believed classmates or teachers supported them to some extent in high school had valuable insights that could help to create similar environments in other schools. In other cases, discussing positive outcomes may have helped to reconcile participation in a study that could stir up somewhat dormant negative feelings. Although more study is needed on HTP in Canadian high schools, including why the phobias persist, research exploring more positive, more complex experiences is essential.

Explaining HTP

The third area explored in this research involved participants' speculations about why HTP harassment persists in B.C. high schools. The major themes that emerged were gender regulation, silence or negative stereotypes about queer people, and bullying as part of the maturation process. Participants' conjectures about causes of HTP provided a context for some of their earlier vignettes about HTP and how people could sometimes change how they were affected by it. Generally, the young people conveyed the feeling that the lofty ideal of diversity is not always extended to those who are, in Kate Bornstein's (1994) wording, "gender outlaws."

Gender Regulation in High Schools
Participants implicitly and directly identified gender variance as a precipitating factor in expressions of HTP. Many were not "out" about their sexual orientation in high school and were read as queer because of their gender variance. We argue that addressing HTP will require reflection and a rethinking of how we understand gender. Bourdieu believes (2001, 24) gender only exists "relationally — [as] a body socially differentiated from the opposite gender." Binary distinctions such as male and female cause us to overlook the commonalities and overlap between valued and devalued identity categories and, in this case, the range of possible gender expressions that elude such simplistic classifications (Bourdieu 2001, 93).

Due to the widespread belief that gender is determined by biological sex (Pascoe 2007), gender and gender expression are usually classified under one of two categories (masculine or feminine). Even biological sex categories (male or female), though, can be seen as social constructs that fail to represent all of the biological possibilities (Fausto-Sterling 2000, 1992). Yet, we hold onto sex and gender categories so tightly that when we encounter bodies that contradict them we find ways to alter the bodies, through incentives, disincentives or even surgery before we alter our frameworks (Middleton 1998). Viewing sex and gender in such strict terms causes us to overlook the wide range of naturally occurring gender identities and expressions and to view those who fail to adhere to hegemonic gender expressions as unnatural.

Negative reactions to gender nonconformity are framed as natural, justified or legitimate. That homophobia and transphobia continue to persist is testament to this process.

Foucault (1977) believes that social norms, including those related to sexuality and gender, become so ingrained that any threat to them is seen as a threat to social order and can result in rejection. Rejection, ostracism and aggression can function as deterrents to certain behaviours, especially gender nonconformity. According to participants, educational institutions are fertile ground for the differentiation, segregation and maltreatment that Bourdieu and Foucault describe, with educators, peers and even architectural structure (washrooms and change rooms) contributing to the gendered division of males and females.

We found that youth who disrupt dominant assumptions linking biological sex, gender and gender expression may be the most affected by HTP bullying. If this is the case, trans and gender-variant youth may be most at-risk of experiencing HTP harassment and perhaps the most direct forms. Wyss (2004, 710) concurs with this:

> Among the queer young people who may have the most difficulty are trans and genderqueer youth. Their relationships with peers are fraught not only with the usual adolescent tensions but also with dynamics introduced when "alternative" gender identities come face to face with the homophobia and transphobia that are rampant in almost all schools.

Elsewhere, we argued for the reframing and renaming of homophobic bullying to emphasize the importance of gender (Haskell and Burtch 2008). In her work, Namaste (1996) has proposed the term "gender-bashing"; we have adopted and used "transphobia" throughout this book. Because of the propensity to associate gender variance with homosexuality, it is difficult to tease out the motivating factors for harassment and to label incidents as either homophobic or transphobic. Often these classifications are made solely on the basis of the sexual and/or gender identity of the person harassed, without critical assessment of the motives or discomfort that lead to the harassment. To reflect the role that gender plays in HTP harassment, we advocate for the use of "transphobia" and apply it beyond situations where trans people are targeted. It is hoped that using the term more broadly may help to call attention to how regulation of gender norms can sometimes intersect with the regulation of sexuality.

Studies on homophobic bullying often refer to or include trans youth but focus on the regulation of sexual orientation rather than gender. Many youth in these studies experienced harassment because of their gender variance; yet, there has been almost no research on the ways that trans and gender-variant youth are affected by transphobia and the propagation of mainstream gender norms in high schools. Here, we call for a closer look at the importance of respecting diversity, including expressions that some of us are uncomfortable with. There is a need, then, to reframe our explorations and to call attention to how strict gender expectations may motivate homophobia and transphobia.

In addition to calling attention to gender as a motivating factor for HTP bullying, participants illustrated the importance of exploring how HTP is experienced differently according to one's gender. Participants said classmates and teachers regulated gender norms related to masculinity more rigorously than they did those related to femininity. Several participants in this study said that "effeminate males" were most likely to experience HTP harassment in Physical Education classes, venues where the associations between aggression, masculinity and heterosexuality are especially clear.

Many would argue that feminist movements have broadened views on how women can behave and appear. Although there is an increasing movement to challenge hegemonic notions of masculinity, one could argue that males are not privy to the same leeway in terms of gender expression that females have gained. As Walls (2008, 62) says, "Heterosexual femininity is not as tied to possessing gender appropriate traits as is heterosexual masculinity." Burn (2000, 3) suggests a different explanation for the prevalence of HTP directed at males over females:

> This difference may be due in part to the general invisibility of lesbianism in comparison to male homosexuality, an invisibility which contributes to an out-of-sight-out-of-mind situation. Worldwide, lesbianism, like female sexuality in general, has been rendered invisible by cultures who naively limit female sexuality to reproduction carried out as part of heterosexual marriage..... We also find more research on male homosexuality, more media portrayals of male homosexuality, more clubs for male homosexuals, and, worldwide, more laws prohibiting male homosexuality than female homosexuality. Historically, women have been considered lower status than men, and it was only through heterosexual marriage that status and economic security could be achieved. This too has contributed to the invisibility of lesbianism, as many lesbian and bisexual women lived heterosexual lives or quiet homosexual ones. In short, the lesbian possibility is largely invisible.

Burn (2000) asserts that acceptable expressions of femininity may not have expanded at all, but that females may be paid little attention when it comes to sexuality (unless it relates to reproductive sex). Burns goes on to argue that hegemonic masculinity may create a space for some queer women in other ways; women who behave in typically masculine ways may be accepted (or at least tolerated) because of the value placed on hegemonic masculinity. Males who are seen as "effeminate" may be more likely to be harassed than gender-variant females, then, because of the gender being portrayed (femininity) rather than the gender of the person who is portraying it.

Burn (2000) argues that hegemonic masculinity is rewarded regardless of who is expressing the characteristics typically associated with it; conversely, feminine characteristics are denigrated. In this study, however, at least some participants who displayed characteristics associated with hegemonic masculinity when perceived as female experienced HTP harassment. Thus, the masculinity hypothesis, or the assertion that femininity is generally undesirable is not supported, at least not in all cases of HTP relayed by participants in this research. Perhaps, as Khayatt (1994, para. 6) posits, "Lesbians experience compulsory heterosexuality as a social invisibility, a silence surrounding their sexual preference, while for gay men, compulsory heterosexuality is often articulated violently."

The HTP harassment that queer young women experience, then, may be invisible for two reasons. First, as Khayatt (1994) states, young queer women seem to be invisible. Second, HTP directed at queer women may take more subtle forms HTP than that directed at their male counterparts. Educators can help, though, by being aware of the various forms of HTP and how they may vary according to gender.

Generally, gender was a significant theme in discussions with participants about their experiences with HTP in high school. Consequently, researchers should approach the topic of HTP bullying with a gendered lens (Walton 2006) and explore how techniques and frequency of HTP harassment vary with the gender of the harasser and the harassed. This research seems to indicate that gender, or gender variance, is a motivating factor for HTP harassment. It would also be useful to gauge whether gender mitigates the effects; that is, do the effects and coping mechanisms vary according to the gender one identifies (or does not identify) as? In addition, because participants identified gender as such an important factor in HTP bullying, school staff may help to reduce levels by, first, expanding students' ideas about masculinity and femininity and, second, by encouraging them to reflect on the usefulness of those categories.

Lack of Information and Misinformation

The second theme related to why HTP persists was a general feeling that homophobia and transphobia stem from ignorance ("not knowing any better") rooted in a lack of exposure to queer people. Participants also believed that misinformation and negative views about homosexuality and gender variance from other social institutions and contexts seep into educational institutions. Urban centres were perceived to be more supportive of queer youth as compared to rural areas where social conservatism and religiosity were believed to be common (see Gray 2009 and Filax 2006 for a discussion of geography, queer youth and social conservatism). Due to the hesitancy of queer people to come out in socially conservative environments, participants also believed youth in rural areas lack positive queer role models and opportunities to engage in productive discussion about issues that affect LGBTTQ youth. Family, media and the law were also mentioned as factors that influence opinions and behaviours in schools and that can work to support or oppress queer people.

Many participants believed that schools could provide a space where prejudices learned at home, including HTP sentiments, can be challenged. Yet, participants said there was frequently a lack of willingness or a hesitancy to discuss issues affecting queer people or even acknowledge the existence of queer youth in some cases. Perhaps students who bully queer youth are trying to enforce some standard of congruence between the set curriculum and the real world they are supposed to reflect. In this case, the silence in classrooms speaks loud and clear, giving students implicit permission to expunge those identities that do not "fit" with their formal curriculum. Some educators themselves may be doing harm to students, or engaging in symbolic violence, by failing to recognize and portray the natural existence of a range of sexual and gender identities.

Bullying As a Normal Part of Maturation

The third and final theme in relation to why HTP happens is related to the maturation process. Several participants saw bullying as a natural occurrence that could be exacerbated by, for instance, problems at home. These young people seemed to indicate that anyone could be "othered" or be made to feel an outsider by another person, who in turn feels like they are an insider or that they fit in. According to Bourdieu and Foucault, though, some people are more likely to be "othered" because they appear or behave in ways that disrupt our ideas about the social world. The experiences of queer youth, who felt they needed to constantly ensure they "fit in" to avoid bullying, seem to support the theorists' suggestions.

Epstein, O'Flynn and Telford (2000/2001, 129) contend that

> there is an official silence about all kinds of sexuality in the vast majority of mainstream schools in Anglophone countries. And even where sexuality is permitted, the form of sexuality allowed is the straightest of straight versions.

They add that teachers who promote a more inclusive, including queer-positive, outlook may jeopardize their very careers (Epstein et al., 141).

They conclude that "the expectation is heterosexuality," whether through behavioural or identity norms. Thus, educational institutions participate in "othering" of people who identify as queer and facilitate in "a narrowing and constraining of heterosexual identities" (Epstein et al., 168)

We are wary of making black-and-white distinctions in which certain sexualities are grouped together as one bloc and contrasted, sharply, with a monolithic grouping of heterosexuals. Lee (2001) makes a crucial point that the process of distinguishing oneself as part of a distinct grouping and distancing oneself from other groupings can occur for people of any sexual orientation. Specifically, her study of lesbians in Britain and North America led her to conclude that there was no clear nexus of butch lesbians and FTMs (female-to-male transsexuals). Instead, "for the lesbians, the social 'other' was heterosexual women and the sexual 'other' was heterosexual men, whilst for the FTMs the social and sexual 'other' was both heterosexual women and lesbians-as-women" (Lee 2001, 356). In general, however, participants' reports support arguments that educational environments are sometimes complicit in, if not encouraging of, the "othering" of queer identities.

Participants reported that queer and trans youth may experience harassment more often than their heterosexual and gender-conforming peers because of teachers' lack of intervention in those cases. Failing to address HTP in schools may actually create an "acceptable" form of bullying and frame queer youth as fair game. Due to its prevalence and the preponderance of outside influences leading to HTP bullying, some participants questioned the extent to which homophobia and transphobia could be challenged in high school. Still, participants were able to make several suggestions on how to make B.C. high schools better places for queer youth.

Reducing HTP: Outing HTP Bullying

The final area explored in this study was how to address homophobia and transphobia in high schools. A small number of participants were sceptical about the extent to which HTP can be reduced in B.C. high schools. As Foucault (1980, 59) says, though, power relations can work in many ways and "power would be a fragile thing if its only function were to repress." Foucault contends that resistance can be found wherever power relations exist. Similarly, Bourdieu (2001, 13–14; emphasis in original) believes "there is always room for a *cognitive struggle* over the meaning of the things of the world and in particular sexual realities." Most participants came up with means of resistance, usually involving raising awareness about HTP bullying and increasing the visibility of queer people in schools.

According to Bourdieu and Foucault, revealing power relations and providing a starting point for resistance to them requires increased awareness and reflexivity in our everyday thinking and sociological thought. For Foucault (1991, 84), this process results in desubjugation, "so that the acts, gestures, discourses that up until then had seemed to go without saying become problematic, difficult, dangerous." Similarly, Hoy explains Bourdieu's thoughts, with which we opened this chapter, as follows:

> Reflexivity of the sociological insight into how asymmetrically the social situation is structured can neutralize the force of the bodily dispositions... to a degree knowledge can be emancipatory. The better we understand the external constraints on our thoughts and action, the more we will see through them and the less effective they will become. (Hoy 1999, 18)

As Swartz (1997, 10) explains, revealing vested interests behind current social hierarchies can call their legitimacy into question and create the possibility for change.

Participants' recommendations provide a starting place to reduce HTP in B.C. high schools. By providing insight into the nature of power relations around sexuality and gender in schools and calling for increased visibility of queer people and awareness of the harassment that affects them in high schools, they set the wheels in motion for change. By volunteering to share their experiences, participants called attention to many invisible aspects of schooling.

To start the process of "desubjugation" in schools, participants said that subtle forms of HTP need to be recognized and addressed. Part of this would involve better teacher training, but it also requires a rethinking of what we currently consider when we think of bullying (Walton 2006). Participants qualified recollections of subtle forms of HTP with statements such as "I didn't necessarily experience bullying, but...." Perhaps our concept of what constitutes bullying should be expanded to include the subtle in-school experiences that had a considerable impact on the participants. Such definitions may reflect the persistent tendency of researchers and school administrators to focus on physical forms of bullying at the expense of others that may be more frequent but no less damaging.

No form of HTP can be addressed without calling attention to the heterosexist and gender-limiting nature of educational institutions. In line with the works of Foucault and Bourdieu, participants thought school staff should encourage reflection on the social categories we often take for granted (and in turn that teacher trainers should do the same). Increasing awareness about the range of sexual and gender identities that exist could help reduce the perception that LGBTTQ identities are unnatural, wrong and deserving of punishment. Martino (2000, 11) has made similar recommendations in his work on masculinities, homophobia and youth, saying, "We have to find ways to help students problematize the whole idea of what is considered to be natural and given and how we have come to understand ourselves in these terms." Yet, participants in this study believed their schools failed to represent LGBTTQ people accurately if at all.

Due to murky policy directives for teachers when it comes to the discussion of queer topics, many feel as though they have no option but to avoid the discussions altogether or to maintain a neutral stance in those that take place (Owens 1998). While some administrators and educators pay lip service to the idea of diversity, they often fail to include a diverse representation of minorities, especially queer people, in their lessons. Silence, however, can sometimes send a more effective message than words and implies that discussing homosexuality and gender variance is inappropriate. In turn, youth may assume the identities associated with those topics are inappropriate. Challenging that conception requires, first, that LGBTTQ be represented in schools and, second, that they be portrayed in a positive light.

As Youdell (2004) states, identities are fragile constructions that come about through discourse. Labels arising from discussions of sexual minorities provide a means of, at the very least, acknowledging the existence and legitimacy of queer identities (Foucault 1984; Youdell 2004). Through this acknowledgement, school administrators gain access to discourses about sexual minorities and, with that, the "symbolic power" to reconstruct the sullied identity conferred upon them (Bourdieu 1991). This reconstruction can be accomplished by speaking about queer people in a positive manner and through the reclaiming of the presently stigmatized labels surrounding queer identities (or as Foucault would say, by creating a reverse discourse) (Penttinen 2008).

Finally, participants stressed the importance of an integrated approach. Discussions about queer people should not be sensational or meant for entertainment; homosexuality and gender variance should be discussed in the same manner as any other topic (Owens 1998). As Youdell (2004) notes, a successful initiative to address HTP bullying must attend to the mundane, day-to-day activities in which homophobic and transphobic attitudes are formed. Researchers also have a role to play in the liberation of queer youth.

Research As Resistance

This research project can be seen as a form of what Foucault termed desubjugation — the starting point for resistance (Lyotard 1987). For example, the findings section answered Foucault and Bourdieu's call for reflexivity by exploring how interactions in B.C. high schools work to both reinforce and undermine social norms. Readers have also been encouraged to think critically about questions of sexuality, gender, power and schooling. The group discussions themselves served as places where critical reflection could take place.

At the beginning of the group discussions, several participants qualified their experiences, saying that the bullying was "not that bad" since they had not been physically hurt. In discussion with others, the frequency of more subtle forms of HTP harassment became apparent. Participants' reflections illustrate how these modes worked to regulate gender expression and sexual orientation. Subtle manifestations of HTP often go unrecognized and students who engage in them are usually not reprimanded. Consequently, these forms may be more effective than overt or physical forms of harassment that are almost always addressed. Some of these insights may not have materialized in one-on-one interviews, which do not allow participants to reflect on others' definitions and experiences and to weigh them against their own. Due to their potential to provide an atmosphere for critical reflections, perhaps small group discussions are something school administrators and teachers should consider as part of their efforts to address HTP bullying in schools.

In the research setting, some may have trepidations about using group formats due to participants' concerns about privacy or the possibility of discomfort in discussing what are sometimes seen as sensitive topics in front of others. In this study, only one participant specifically said the group format made it tough for him to open up about his experiences. After the discussion, however, this participant actually sought Rebecca out to tell her how much he enjoyed having the opportunity to be heard. In fact, he continued to tell her more about the harassment he had endured and the ways it had affected him both positively and negatively.

Other researchers working with queer youth have appreciated the benefits of group formats. Speaking of group work with young male-to-female sex workers, Klein (1999, 101) says:

> Through the examples of others, members learn about themselves, as they share commonalities of their experience and feel the connection to their peers. The positive achievement provides group members with direction and feelings of hope about the future.

Group work and discussions could be useful in high schools as well. Using a small group format to discuss the various manifestations of homophobia and transphobia in high schools and how they may affect queer (and straight or gender-conforming) youth may be beneficial to those wishing to address HTP. Discussing even hypothetical situations in a group format can help students to identify harmful behaviours or actions that otherwise may not have registered as such. Expressing their own and hearing others' opinions on what "counts" as bullying and HTP may encourage youth to at least be aware that others believe their language or behaviours are hurtful, even if the youth do not see it that way themselves.

Conclusion

"A Better Place"

As we wrote this concluding section, a Vancouver newspaper reported on an alleged gay bashing at a prom held specifically for gay young people. Homophobia is not limited by age, however (Hainsworth 2009). Other headlines in Vancouver in 2009 covered the attack of a gay man whose attacker later said, "He deserved it. The faggot touched me. I'm not a fag" (Hansen 2009). Early in 2008, Jason Smith was bashed in the West End of Vancouver as he walked along Davie Street, one of the most prominent gay neighbourhoods in Canada, while holding hands with a male friend. As they walked, four young men approached them hurling anti-gay epithets ("Apparent Gay Bashing" 2008). Though Smith walked away from the group, the men pursued him and one punched him in the face, breaking his jaw and knocking him unconscious. Thanks to bystanders who intervened and called police, the attack stopped and the police apprehended a suspect soon after.

Certainly these attacks are not unique; according to the 2004 General Social Survey, gay men and lesbians reported experiencing violence at more than two times, and bisexuals, four times, the rate that heterosexual people did (Beauchamp 2004, 8). This difference held even when variables that often predispose people to violence (age, lifestyle, income and so forth) were controlled for. Similarly, in *Pink Blood: Homophobic Violence in Canada*, Janoff (2005) details brutal attacks of over one hundred LGBTTQ people in Canada since 1990. That recent bashings of gay men in Vancouver happened in public, in a known queer space, and in front of bystanders, illustrates the very real dangers that LGBTTQ people face.

We suspect that the men who allegedly committed the assaults did not one day wake up and decide that they hated gay men enough to warrant physically attacking one. Instead, the attacks were probably the culmination of years of exposure to homophobia and transphobia that had gone unaddressed, sending the message that queer people are acceptable targets and that, when targeted, there are no repercussions, at least not for the attacker(s). Subtle forms of HTP lead to more visible and physical forms of violence because they foster the belief that queer people deserve to be punished, especially those who are brave enough to "flaunt" their sexuality and gender variance in public. Given the role those other forms of bullying play in creating an environment where physical harassment can and does happen, we cannot help but wonder what has not been reported.

In the wake of one of the bashings described above, Jennifer Breakspear, the current executive director at Qmunity (formerly The Centre), a community centre in Vancouver for LGTB people and their allies, stated that queer people often do not report harassment they experience because of mistrust of the police (Wintonyk 2008). In fact, Qmunity and the Vancouver Police Department teamed up in an unprecedented partnership to improve relations between the queer community and the police through a series of public forums in November 2008. Perhaps least likely to come to police attention are incidents involving HTP in schools, which are often viewed as the purview of school staff, not law enforcement. Rather than protecting them, the law requires queer youth (up to the age of sixteen) to enter an environment that can be perceived as threatening, and that may in fact be dangerous both physically and mentally, due to the lack of acceptance of homosexuality and gender variance in schools (Owens 1998).

Participants recalled several physical and verbal attacks that happened both off and on school property, only one of which came to the attention of police and certainly none of which were reported in the press. Yet Owens (1998) reports that adolescents are the most likely of any age group to commit acts of violence against queer people. What is dubbed a hate crime after receiving vehement response by police, media and the public is often downplayed as "kids being kids" (or usually "boys being boys") in the school context. When addressed, HTP harassment in educational institutions is often treated as "bad behaviour" or the result of one "bad seed," yet the same behaviours in a different context are labelled as hate crimes. Why the discrepancy?

While schools disseminate common knowledge, they also "teach" students to conform to the taken-for-granted roles and norms of society. Schools thus generate and perpetuate the perception of queer people as problematic rather than identifying homophobic and transphobic attitudes as the problems in need of addressing (Flowers and Buston 2001). Consequently, ongoing efforts to create "safe schools" where diversity is respected and valued send a contradictory message (Walton 2006); the failure of schools to challenge societal norms encourages bullying behaviours directed toward those who contravene them, especially students perceived to be queer. Yet, when people police sexual and gender boundaries outside of the school context we accuse them of hate, identifying the homophobia and transphobia underpinning their actions. Perhaps this is a case of little too late; perhaps we cannot blame people for internalizing the lessons they learned in high school, even if those lessons are informal or "hidden."

Our participants shared their experiences, both positive and negative, as queer youth in B.C. high schools. Three of sixteen participants classified their experiences as positive; yet, several others said their experiences were negative and even horrible. Clearly, there is room for improvement. Regardless of how participants interpreted their experiences, their recommendations were the same: queer people, and especially queer youth, need to be acknowledged in schools through inclusion in the curriculum, intervention in homophobic and transphobic behaviours (including subtle forms), and creation of an open dialogue with and about queer youth.

These youth are not alone in their call to action. Recent research (Darwich 2008; Elze 2005; Espelage et al. 2008) shows how having supportive teachers, peers and parents can help queer youth to develop positive self-identities and mediate against the homophobia they encounter not only in schools, but in society in general. Phoenix said this about the lasting impact the support she received in high school:

> It's helped me to realize also that I can help others too. Like... [having] an instructor and administration and my friends support me... when I was learning about myself and just kind of coming out and all that stuff, seeing how they supported me has helped me to support others in progression. So I think that's kind of helped to make, not just me better, but hopefully, in some small way, make the world a better place too. (queer, androgynous)

References

"Abbotsford School Board Permits Controversial Social Justice Elective." (2009, February 10). *CBC News*. Retrieved August 8, 2009, from <cbc.ca/canada/british-columbia/story/2009/02/10/bc-abbotsford-elective-course.html>.

Angelides, S. (2005). "The Emergence of the Paedophile in the Late Twentieth Century." *Australian Historical Studies, 37*(26), 272–95.

"Apparent Gay Bashing in Vancouver Investigated as Hate Crime." (2008, September, 28). *CBC News*. Retrieved September 29, 2008, from <cbc.ca/canada/british-columbia/story/2008/09/28/bc-hate-crime.html>.

Arsenault, L.A. (2000). "High School Confidential: Lesbian Students Speak of Public High School Experiences in Nova Scotia." Unpublished master's thesis, Faculty of Education, Acadian University, Wolfville, NS.

Artz, L., and B. Murphy. (2000). *Cultural Hegemony in the United States.* Thousand Oaks, CA: Sage.

Beauchamp, D. (2004). *Sexual Orientation and Victimization.* Ottawa, ON: Canadian Centre for Justice Statistics.

Becker, H. (2007). *Writing for Social Scientists: How to Start and Finish Your Thesis, Book, or Article* (2nd ed.). Chicago, IL: University of Chicago Press.

Beeby, D. (2010, March 2). "Immigration Minister Pulled Gay Rights From Citizenship Guide, Document Shows." *Globe and Mail.* Retrieved March 14, 2010, from <theglobeandmail.com/news/politics/immigration-minister-pulled-gay-rights-from-citizenship-guide-documents-show/article1486935/>.

Bellaart, D. (2010, February 10). "Parents of Nanaimo Teen Who Committed Suicide Say School Bullying Policy Ineffective." *The Province.* Retrieved March 10, 2010, from <theprovince.com/technology/Parents+Nanaimo+teen+committed+suicide+school+bullying+policy+ineffective/2537333/story.html>.

Birden, S. (2005). *Rethinking Sexual Identity in Education.* Lanham, MD: Rowan and Littlefield Publishers.

Blumenfeld, W. (1992). *Homophobia: How We All Pay the Price.* Boston, MA: Beacon Press.

Blumenfeld, W., and D. Raymond. (1993). *Looking at Gay and Lesbian Life* (2nd ed.). Boston, MA: Beacon Press.

Board of School Trustees of School District No. 44 (North Vancouver) v. Jubran et al., 2003, BCSC 6. Retrieved March 27, 2010, from <canlii.org/en/bc/bcsc/doc/2003/2003bcsc6/2003bcsc6.html>.

Bochenek, M., and A. Widney. (2001). "Hatred in The Hallways: Violence and Discrimination Against Lesbian, Gay, Bisexual, and Transgender Students in U.S. Schools." New York: Human Rights Watch. Retrieved November 15, 2007, from <hrw.org/reports/2001/uslgbt>.

Bornstein, K. (1994). *Gender Outlaw: On Men, Women, and the Rest of Us.* New York, London: Routledge.

Bourdieu, P. (1990/1980). *The Logic of Practice* (R. Nice, Trans.). Cambridge, UK: Polity Press.

———. (1991). *Language and Symbolic Power* (J. Thomson, Ed.; G. Raymond, Trans.). Cambridge, MA: Polity Press in Association with Basil Blackwell.

———. (2000/1997). *Pascalian Meditations* (R. Nice, Trans.). Cambridge, UK: Polity Press.

———. (2001/1998). *Masculine Domination* (R. Nice, Trans.). Cambridge, UK: Polity Press.

Bourdieu, P., and J.C. Passeron. (1990/1970). *Reproduction in Education, Society, and Culture* (R. Nice, Trans.). London; Newbury Park, CA: Sage.

Bryers, M. (2008, August 21–28). "Canada Isn't Rushing to Defend Human Rights." *Georgia Straight.* Retrieved July 11, 2010, from <straight.com/article-158325/canada-isnt-rushing-defend-human-rights>.

Burgess, C. (1999). "Internal and External Stress Factors Associated with the Identity Development of Transgendered Youth." In G. Mallon (Ed.), *Social Services with Transgendered Youth* (pp. 35–48). Binghamton, NY: Harrington Park Press.

Burn, S. (2000). "Heterosexuals' Use of 'Fag' and 'Queer' to Deride One Another: A Contributor to Heterosexism and Stigma." *Journal of Homosexuality, 40*(2), 1–11.

Buston, K., and G. Hart. (2001). "Heterosexism and Homophobia in Scottish School Sex Education: Exploring the Nature of the Problem." *Journal of Adolescence, 24*(1), 95–109.

Callaghan, T. (2007). *That's So Gay! Homophobia in Canadian Catholic Schools.* Germany: VDM Verlag Dr. Mueller e.K.

"Canada Upholds Gay Marriage Law." (2006, December 8). *BBC News.* Retrieved August 29, 2009, from <news.bbc.co.uk/2/hi/Americas/6219914.stm>.

"Catholic Schools Reject Participation in Homophobia Survey." (2008, January 25). *CBC News.* Retrieved November 3, 2008, from <cbc.ca/canada/toronto/story/2008/01/25/egale-survey.html>.

Chamberlain v. Surrey School District No. 36, [2002] 4 S.C.R. 710, 2002 SCC 86.

Citizenship and Immigration Canada. (2007). "Immigration Overview: Permanent Residents and Temporary Foreign Workers and Students." Retrieved August 24, 2008, from <cic.gc.ca/english/resources/statistics/facts2007/foreword.asp>.

Cochrane, D., and M. Morrison. (2008). "How Safe and Welcoming Are Saskatchewan Secondary Schools for LGBQ Youth? A Preliminary Report on Student Perceptions." Paper presented at Breaking the Silence conference, University of Saskatchewan, Saskatchewan.

Collins, P. (2000). *Black Feminist Thought: Knowledge, Consciousness, and the Politics of Empowerment.* New York: Routledge.

Connell, R.W., and J. Messerschmidt. (2005). "Hegemonic Masculinity: Rethinking the Concept." *Gender and Society, 19*(6), 829–59.

Connell, R. (2005). "Growing Up Masculine: Rethinking the Significance of Adolescence in the Making of Masculinities." *Irish Journal of Sociology, 14*(2), 11–28.

Continuing Legal Education Society of British Columbia. (2005). "BCCA: North Vancouver School Board Liable for Homophobic Harassment of Student." Retrieved February 12, 2006, from <cle.bc.ca/CLE/Stay+Current/Collection/2005/4/05-bcca-jubran?practiceAreaMessage=trueandpracticeArea=Administrative%20Law>.

Cook and Warren v. Ministry of Education, 2003 BCHRT 25.

Corren and Corren v. B.C. (Ministry of Education) (No. 2), 2005 BCHRT 497.

D'Augelli, A. (1998). "Developmental Implications of Victimization of Lesbian, Gay, and Bisexual Youths." In G.M. Herek (Ed.), *Stigma and Sexual Orientation: Understanding Prejudice Against Lesbians, Gay Men, and Bisexuals* (pp. 187–210). Thousand Oaks, CA: Sage.

D'Augelli, A., S. Hershberger, and N. Pilkington. (2001). "Suicidality Patterns and Sexual Orientation-Related Factors among Lesbian, Gay, and Bisexual Youth." *Suicide and Life Threatening Behavior, 35*(6), 646–60.

Darwich, L. (2008). "Lesbian, Gay, Bisexual, and Questioning Adolescents: Their Social Experiences and the Role of Supportive Adults in High School." Unpublished master's thesis, Faculty of Education, University of British Columbia, Vancouver, BC.

Denike, M., S. Renshaw, and C. Rowe. (2003). "Transgender and Women's Substantive Equality Discussion Paper." *National Association of Women and the Law*. Retrieved March 10, 2008, from <72.14.253.104/search?q=cache:gk6oVfkJshYJ:www.nawl. ca/ns/en/documents/Pub_Report_Trans03_en.doc+transgender+case+law+Ca nadaandhl=enandct=clnkandcd=1andgl=caandclient=firefox-a>.

Devor, H. (1989). *Gender Blending: Confronting the Limits of Duality*. Bloomington, IN: Indiana University Press.

DiPlacido, J. (1998). "Minority Stress among Lesbians, Gay Men, and Bisexuals: A Consequence of Heterosexism, Homophobia, and Stigmatization." In G. Herek (Ed.), *Stigma and Sexual Orientation: Understanding Prejudice against Lesbians, Gay Men, and Bisexuals* (pp. 138–59). Thousand Oaks, CA: Sage Publications.

Dorias, M., and S. Lajeunesse. (2004). *Dead Boys Can't Dance: Sexual Orientation, Masculinity, and Suicide* (P. Tremblay, Trans.). Montreal, QC: McGill-Queen's University Press.

Douglas, N., I. Warwick, S. Kemp, G. Whitty, and P. Aggleton. (1999). "Homophobic Bullying in Secondary Schools in England and Wales — Teachers' Experiences." *Health Education, 99*(2), 53–60.

Dunn, W. (2004). *Public Policy Analysis: An Introduction* (3rd ed.). Upper Saddle River, NJ: Pearson Prentice Hall.

Dwyer, V., and S. Farran. (1997). "Fighting Homophobia at School." *Xtra*. Retrieved August 16, 2009, from <egale.ca/index.asp?lang=Eandmenu=33anditem=169>.

Edwards, T. (2006). *Cultures of Masculinity*. New York, NY: Routledge.

Egale Canada. (2009). "Youth Speak Up About Homophobia and Transphobia: The First National Climate Survey on Homophobia in Canadian Schools Phase One Report." Retrieved July 11, 2010, from <http://climatesurvey.ca/report/ClimateSurvey-PhaseOneReport.pdf>.

El-Bushra, J. (2000). "Transforming Conflict: Some Thoughts on a Gendered Understanding of Conflict Processes." In S. Jacobs, R. Jacobson and J. Marchbank (Eds.), *States of Conflict: Gender, Violence and Resistance* (pp. 66–82). New York: Zed Books.

Elze, D. (2005). "Research with Sexual Minority Youths: Where Do We Go from Here?" *Journal of Gay and Lesbian Social Services, 18*(2), 73–99.

Epstein, D., S. O'Flynn, and D. Telford. (2000/2001). "'Othering' Education: Sexualities, Silences, and Schooling." *Review of Research in Education, 25*(1), 127–79.

Espelage, D., S. Aragon, M. Birkett, and B. Koenig. (2008). "Homophobic Teasing, Psychological Outcomes and Sexual Orientation among High School Students: What Influence Do Parents and School Have?" *School Psychology Review, 37*(2), 202–16.

Faubert, J., and R. Haskell. (2006, October). "Sexual (Ab)normality and Sexual "(Dis) Orientation Discourse in Dangerous Offender Hearings." Paper presented at Sex at SFU Colloquium, Simon Fraser University, Burnaby, BC.

Fausto-Sterling. (2000). *Sexing the Body: Gender Politics and the Construction of Sexuality.* New York: Basic Books.

Faulkner, E. (2007). "Homophobic Hate Propaganda in Canada." *Journal of Hate Studies, 5*(63), 63–97.

Filax, G. (2006) *Queer Youth in the Province of the Severely Normal.* Vancouver, BC: University of British Columbia Press.

Flowers, P., and K. Buston. (2001). "'I Was Terrified of Being Different': Exploring Gay Men's Accounts of Growing-Up in a Heterosexist Society." *Journal of Adolescence, 24*(1), 51–65.

Forde, J. (2006). "Homophobia." In D. Gerstner (Ed.), *Routledge International Encyclopedia of Queer Culture.* New York: Routledge.

Foucault, M. (1977/1975). *Discipline and Punish: The Birth of the Prison* (A. Sheridan, Trans.). New York: Pantheon Books.

———. (1980). *Power/Knowledge: Selected Interviews and Other Writings, 1972–1977* (C. Gordon, Ed.; C. Gordon, L. Marshall, J. Mepham, and K. Soper, Trans.). New York: Pantheon Books.

———. (1984). "Nietzsche, Genealogy, History." In P. Rabinow (Ed.), *The Foucault Reader.* New York: Pantheon Books.

———. (1990/1976). *The History of Sexuality, Volume 1* (R. Hurley, Trans.). New York: Vintage Books.

———. (1991). "Questions of Method." In Burchell, G., Gordon, C., and Miller, P. (Eds). *The Foucault Effect: Studies in Governmentality with Two Lectures and an Interview with Michel Foucault* (pp. 73–86). Chicago, IL: University of Chicago Press.

———. (1996/1984). "The Concern for Truth" (Interview by F. Ewald; J. Johnston, Trans.). In S. Lotringer (Ed.), *Foucault Live: Collected Interviews, 1961–1984* (pp. 455–64). New York: Semiotext(e).

Fox, K. (2004) *Watching the English: The Hidden Rules of English Behaviour.* London: Hodder and Stoughton.

Freedman, E. (1987). "'Uncontrolled Desires': The Response to the Sexual Psychopath, 1920–1960." *Journal of American History, 74,* 83–106.

Gagné, P., and R. Tewksbury. (1998). "Conformity Pressures and Gender Resistance among Transgendered Individuals." *Social Problems, 45*(1), 81–101.

Gagné, P., R. Tewksbury, and D. McGaughey. (1997). "Coming Out and Crossing Over: Identity Formation and Proclamation in Transgender Community." *Gender and Society, 11*(4), 478–508.

GALE BC. (n.d.). "About GALE." Retrieved February 7, 2006, from <galebc.org/main. htm>.

Gay and Lesbian Medical Association. (2001). "Healthy People 2010 Companion Document for Lesbian, Gay, Bisexual, and Transgender (LGBT) Health." San Francisco, CA.

"Gay Pride Cash May Have Led to Demotion of MP." (2009, June 7). *CTV News.* Retrieved August 29, 2009, from, <ctv.ca/servlet/ArticleNews/story/CT-VNews/20090707/pride_tories_090707/20090707?hub=TopStories>.

Gender Public Advocacy Coalition. (2006). "50 under 30: Masculinity and the War on America's Youth." Retrieved February 19, 2008, from <gpac.org/50under30/50u30.pdf>.

Gilbert, M. (2004). "The Health of Lesbian, Gay, Bisexual, Transgendered, Two-Spirited and Questioning Youth in British Columbia and the Influence of School." Retrieved February 3, 2006, from <galebc.org/The%20health%20of%20GLBT.pdf>.

"Glossary." (2009). *PFLAG Canada*. Retrieved August 27, 2009, from <pflagcanada.ca/en/aboutframe-e.asp?aboutframe=glossary-e.html%23transsexual>.

Goodenow, C., L. Szalacha, and K. Westheimer. (2006). "School Support Groups, Other School Factors, and the Safety of Sexual Minority Adolescents." *Psychology in Schools, 43*(5), 573–89.

Grace, A. (2005). "Lesbian, Gay, Bisexual, and Trans-Identified (LGBT) Teachers and Students and the Post-Charter Quest for Ethical and Just Treatment in Canadian Schools." *Proceedings of Building Inclusive Schools: A Search for Solutions.* Ottawa, ON: Canadian Teachers Federation. Retrieved July 11, 2010, from <teachers.ab.ca/For%20Members/Professional%20Development/Diversity%20and%20Human%20Rights/Sexual%20Orientation/Publications/Articles/Pages/LGBT.aspx>.

Grace, A. and K. Wells. (2005). "The Marc Hall Prom Predicament: Queer Individual Rights v. Institutional Church Rights in Canadian Public Education." *Canadian Journal of Education, 28*(3), 237–70.

Gramsci, A. (1971). *Selections from the Prison Notebooks of Antonio Gramsci* (Q. Hoare and G. Smith, Eds.). New York: International Publishers.

Gray, M. (2009). *Out in the Country: Youth, Media, and Queer Visibility in Rural America.* New York: NYU Press.

Hainsworth, J. (2009, July 20). "Gaybashing Mars Queer Prom." *Xtra West.* Retrieved August 29, 2009, from <xtra.ca/public/Vancouver/Gaybashing_mars_Queer_Prom-7207.aspx>.

Hall (Litigation guardian of) v. Powers [2002] O.J, No. 1803.

Hansen, D. (2009, March 18). "Gay Community Rallies Against Vancouver Pub Attack." *Xtra West.* Retrieved August 29, 2009, from <vancouversun.com/news/community+rallies+against+attack/1399948/story.html>.

Haskell, R. (2008). "A 'Gentle' Violence? Former Students' Experiences with Homophobia and Transphobia." Unpublished master's thesis, School of Criminology, Simon Fraser University, Burnaby, BC. Available at <ir.lib.sfu.ca/bitstream/1892/10582/1/etd4272.pdf>.

Haskell, R., and B. Burtch. (2008). "Beyond Black and White: Queer Youth and Gender Binaries in British Columbia High Schools." Paper presented at the Canadian Sociological Association 43rd Annual Meeting, Vancouver, BC.

Hasselriis, K. (2009). "Alberta Bill Threatens Lessons on Gay Life." *Xtra.* Retrieved August 16, 2009, from <xtra.ca/public/National/Alberta_bill_threatens_lessons_on_gay_life-6816.aspx>.

Herek, G. (1992). "Psychological Heterosexism and Anti-Gay Violence: The Social Psychology of Bigotry and Bashing." In G. Herek and K. Berrill (Eds.), *Hate Crimes: Confronting Violence against Lesbians and Gay Men* (pp. 60–80). Newbury Park, CA: Sage.

Hetrick, E., and A. Martin. (1984). "Ego-dystonic Homosexuality." In. E. Hetrick and T. Stein (Eds.), *Psychotherapy with Homosexuals* (pp. 2–21). Washington, DC: American Psychiatric Press.

Howlett, M., and M. Ramesh. (2003). *Studying Public Policy: Policy Cycles and Policy Subsystems.* Toronto, ON: Oxford University Press.

Hoy, D.C. (1999). "Critical Resistance: Foucault and Bourdieu." In G. Weiss and H.F. Haber (Eds.), *Perspectives on Embodiment: The Intersections of Nature and Culture* (pp. 3–22). New York: Routledge.

———. (2004). *Critical Resistance: From Post-Structuralism to Post-Critique.* Cambridge, MA: MIT Press.

Human Rights Code, RSBC 1996 U.S.C. Chapter 210 (1996). Retrieved February 12, 2006, from <qp.gov.bc.ca/statreg/Stat/H/96210_01.htm>.

Janoff, V.D. (2005). *Pink Blood: Homophobic Violence in Canada.* Toronto, ON: University of Toronto Press.

Karslake, D. (Director/ Producer). (2007). *For the Bible Tells Me So* [Motion Picture]. New York: First Run Features.

Kenway, J., and L. Fitzclarence. (1997). "Masculinity, Violence and Schooling: Challenging 'Poisonous Pedagogies.'" *Gender and Education, 9*(1), 117–34.

Khayatt, D. (1994). "Surviving School as a Lesbian." *Gender and Education, 6*(1), 47–62. Retrieved July 11, 2010, from <informaworld.com/smpp/content~db= all~content=a739499779>.

Kimmel, M. (1994). "Masculinity as Homophobia: Fear, Shame, and Silence in the Construction of Gender Identity." In H. Brod and M. Kaufam (Eds.), *Theorizing Masculinities* (pp. 274–88). Thousand Oaks, CA: Sage.

Kimmel, M., and M. Mahler. (2003). "Adolescent Masculinity, Homophobia and Violence." *American Behavioural Scientist, 46*(10), 1439–-58.

Kitts, R. (2005). "Gay Adolescents and Suicide: Understanding the Association." *Adolescence, 40*(159), 621–28.

Kitzinger, C., and S. Wilkinson. (1994). "Virgins and Queers: Rehabilitating Heterosexuality?" *Gender and Society, 8*(3), 444–63.

Klages, M. (1997). "Queer Theory." Retrieved October 27, 2004, from <colorado.edu/ English/ENGL2012Klages/queertheory.html>.

Klein, R. (1999). "Group Work Practice with Transgendered Male to Female Sex Workers." In G. Mallon (Ed.), *Social Services with Transgendered Youth* (pp. 65–82). Binghamton, NY: Harrington Park Press.

Kosciw, J.G., and E.M. Diaz. (2006). "The 2005 National School Climate Survey: The Experiences of Lesbian, Gay, Bisexual and Transgender Youth in Our Nation's Schools." New York: Gay, Lesbian, and Straight Education Network [GLSEN].

Kosciw, J., E. Diaz, and E. Greytak. (2008). "The 2007 National School Climate Survey: The Experiences of Lesbian, Gay, Bisexual and Transgender Youth in Our Nation's Schools." New York: Gay, Lesbian, and Straight Education Network [GLSEN].

Leavitt, G. (1999). "Criminological Theory As an Art Form: Implications for Criminal Justice Policy." *Crime and Delinquency, 45*(3), 389–99.

Lee, T. (2001). Trans (Re)Lations: Lesbian and Female to Male Transsexual Accounts of Identity. *Women's Studies International Forum, 24*(3), 347–57.

Lerat, G. (2004). "Two-Spirit Youth Speak Out! Analysis of the Needs Assessment Tool." Urban Native Youth Association. Retrieved September 19, 2008, from

<unya.bc.ca/Two%20Spirit%20Final%20Report%20March%202004.pdf>.

Leung, H. (2008). *Undercurrents: Queer Culture and Postcolonial Hong Kong.* Vancouver, BC: University of British Columbia Press.

Levy, D. (2007) "Hegemonic Masculinity." In M. Flood, J. Gardiner, B. Pease and K. Pringle (Eds.), *International Encyclopedia of Men and Masculinities.* New York: Routledge.

Li, Q. 2006. "Cyberbullying in Schools: A Research of Gender Difference." *School Psychology Inernational, 27*(2), 157–170.

Lindsay Jane Willow v. Halifax Regional School Board, Dr. Gordon Young, and John Orlando, 2006, NSHRC. Retrieved November 7, 2008, from <gov.ns.ca/human-rights/decisions/2006WillowOpinionMay906.pdf>.

Lombardi, E., R. Wilchins, D. Priesing, and D. Malouf. (2001). "Gender Violence: Transgender Experiences with Violence and Discrimination." *Journal of Homosexuality, 42*(1), 89–101.

Loutzenheiser, L., and L. MacIntosh. (2004). "Citizenship, Sexualities, and Education." *Theory into Practice, 42*(2), 151–58.

Luhtanen, M. (2005). "Challenging Equality: Human Rights for Trans-Identified Communities." *LawNow.* Retrieved August 25, 2008, from <findarticles.com/p/articles/mi_m0OJX/is_1_30/ai_n25121531>.

Lyotard, J. (1987). "Questions of Method: An Interview with Michel Foucault." In K. Baynes, J. Bohman and T. McCarthy (Eds.), *After Philosophy: End or Transformation?* (pp. 100–117). Cambridge, MA: MIT Press.

Mahan, W., K. Varjas, B. Dew, J. Meyers, A. Singh, M. Marshall, and E. Graybill. (2006). "School and Community Services Providers' Perspectives on Gay, Lesbian, and Questioning Bullying." *Journal of LGBT Issues in Counselling, 1*(2), 45–66.

Mallon, G. (1999). "Practice with Transgendered Children." In G. Mallon (Ed.), *Social Services with Transgendered Youth* (pp. 49–65). Binghamton, NY: Harrington Park Press.

———. (2000). "Knowledge for Practice with Transgendered Persons." *Journal of Gay and Lesbian Social Services, 10*(3), 1–18.

Marinoble, R. (1998). "Homosexuality: A Blind Spot in the School Mirror." *Professional School Counselling, 1*(3), 4–8. Retrieved July 11, 2010, from <web.ebscohost.com.proxy.lib.sfu.ca/ehost/detail?vid=3&hid=106&sid=349b4ca7-42db-4286-b8d3-8f4966ceaa76%40sessionmgr110&bdata=JnNpdGU9ZWhvc3QtbGl2ZQ%3d%3d#db=aph&AN=288436>.

Martino, W. (2000). "Policing Masculinities: Investigating the Role of Homophobia and Heteronormativity in the Lives of Adolescent School Boys." *Journal of Men's Studies, 8*(2), 213–36.

Mayencourt, L., B. Locke, and W. McMahon. (2003). "Facing Our Fear — Accepting Responsibility: A Report of the Safe Schools Task Force." *Safe Schools Task Force.* Victoria, BC: Government of British Columbia.

Maynard, S. (2001). "The Maple Leaf (Gardens) Forever: Sex, Canadian Historians and National History." *Journal of Canadian Studies, 36*(2), 70-105.

McCreary Centre Society. (1999). "Being Out — Lesbian, Gay, Bisexual, and Transgender Youth in B.C.: An Adolescent Health Survey." Vancouver, BC: McCreary Centre Society.

Messerschmidt, J. (2000). *Nine Lives: Adolescent Masculinities, the Body, and Violence.*

Boulder, CO: Westview Press.

———. (2007). "Goodbye to the Sex-Gender Distinction, Hello to Embodied Gender: On Masculinities, Bodies and Violence." In L. Ferber, K. Holcomb and T. Wentling (Eds.), *Sex, Gender, and Sexuality: The New Basics* (pp. 71–88). New York: Oxford University Press.

Meyer, E. (2006). "Gendered Harassment in North America: Recognising Homophobia and Heterosexism among Students." In Claudia Mitchell and Fiona Leach (Eds.), *Combating Gender Violence in and around Schools* (pp. 43–50). UK: Trentham Books.

———. (2007a, April). "Bullying and Harassment in Secondary Schools: A Critical Feminist Analysis of the Gaps, Overlaps, and Implications from a Decade of Research." Paper presented at the annual meeting of the American Educational Research Association, Chicago, IL.

———. (2007b, April). "Gendered Harassment in High School: Understanding Teachers' (Non)Intervention." Paper presented at the annual meeting of the American Educational Research Association, Chicago, IL.

———. (2008). "A Feminist Reframing of Bullying and Harassment: Transforming Schools Through Critical Pedagogy." *McGill Journal of Education, 43*(1), 33–48.

Meyer, I., and L. Dean. (1998). "Internalized Homophobia, Intimacy, and Sexual Behaviour among Gay and Bisexual Men." In G. Herek (Ed.), *Stigma and Sexual Orientation: Understanding Prejudice Against Lesbians, Gay Men, and Bisexuals* (pp. 97–107). Thousand Oaks, CA: Sage Publications.

Middleton, S. (1998). *Disciplining Sexuality: Foucault, Life Histories, and Education.* New York: Columbia University.

Miller, A. (1990). *For Your Own Good: Hidden Cruelty in Child-Rearing and the Roots of Violence.* New York: Noonday Press.

Monette, P. (1995) "The Politics of Silence." In N. Baldwin and D. Osen (Eds.), *The Writing Life: National Book Award Winners* (pp. 199–213). New York: Random House.

———. (2004/1992). *Becoming a Real Man: Half a Life Story.* New York: Perennial Classics.

Moran, J. (2005, June 16). "Jeremy Dias Creates Scholarship with Rights Settlement." *Xtra Capital.* Retrieved March 4, 2008, from <xtra.ca/public/viewstory.aspx?SESSIONID=9415bcae-1578-448f-9ec5-a5fa9b09d855andAFF_TYPE=2andSTORY_ID=617andPUB_TEMPLATE_ID=2>.

Murray and Peter Corren Foundation. (n.d.). "History on the Establishment of the Foundation." Retrieved September 18, 2008, from <corren.ca>.

Namaste, K. (1996). "Genderbashing: Sexuality, Gender, and the Regulation of Public Space." *Environment and Planning D: Society and Space, 14,* 221–40.

Nayak, A., and M.J. Kehily. (1996). "Playing It Straight: Masculinities, Homophobia, and Schooling." *Journal of Gender Studies, 5*(2), 211–30.

Norris, C. (1990). *What's Wrong with Postmodernism: Critical Theory and the Ends of Philosophy.* Hemel Hempstead, UK: Harvester Wheatsheaf.

———. (1992). *Uncritical Theory: Postmodernism, Intellectuals and the Gulf War.* London, UK: Lawrence and Wishart.

O'Connor, A. (1995). "Breaking the Silence: Writing About Gay, Lesbian, and Bisexual Teenagers." In G. Unks (Ed.), *The Gay Teen: Educational Practice and Theory for*

Lesbian, Gay, and Bisexual Adolescents (pp. 13–16). New York: Routledge.

Olweus, D. (1993). *Bullying at School: What We Know and What We Can Do.* Cambridge, MA: Blackwell Publishers.

Owens, R. (1998). *Queer Kids: The Challenges and Promises for Lesbian, Gay, and Bisexual Youth.* New York: Haworth Press.

Park, J. (2007). "Why I Don't Want to Marry (And Why I Don't Want You too Either)." In R. Labonte and L. Schimel (Eds.), *First Person Queer: Who We Are (So Far)* (pp. 108–12). Vancouver, BC: Arsenal Pulp Press.

Pascoe, C.J. (2007). *Dude, You're a Fag: Masculinity and Sexuality in High School.* Berkeley, CA: University of California Press.

Pazos, S. (1999). "Practice with Female-To-Male Transgendered Youth." In G. Mallon (Ed.), *Social Services with Transgendered Youth* (pp. 65–82). Binghamton, NY: Harrington Park Press.

Pegura et al. v. School District No. 36, 2003 BCHRT 53.

Penttinen, E. (2008). *Globalization, Prostitution and Sex-Trafficking: Corporeal Politics.* New York: Routledge.

Peters, E. (1967). *Greek Philosophical Terms: A Historical Lexicon.* New York: University Press.

PFLAG Canada. (2009). PFLAG Canada Index. Available at <pflagcanada.ca/en/index-e.asp>.

Pfohl, S. (1985). *Images of Deviance and Social Control: A Sociological History.* New York: McGraw-Hill.

Radkowsky, M., and L. Siegel. (1997). "The Gay Adolescent: Stressors, Adaptations, and Psychosocial Interventions." *Clinical Psychology Review, 17*(2), 191–216.

Redman, P. (2000). "'Tarred with the Same Brush': Homophobia and the Role of the Unconscious in School-Based Cultures of Masculinity." *Sexualities, 3*(4), 483–99.

Renold, E. (2002). "Presumed Innocence: (Hetero)Sexual, Heterosexist and Homophobic Harassment Among Primary Schools Girls And Boys." *Childhood, 9*(4), 415–34.

Rivers, I. (2004). "Recollections of Bullying at School and Their Long-Term Implications for Lesbian, Gay Men, and Bisexual." *Crisis: The Journal of Crisis Intervention and Suicide Prevention, 25*(4), 169–75.

Roesler, T., and R. Deisher. (1972). "Youthful Male Homosexuality: Homosexual Experience and the Process of Developing Homosexual Identity in Males Aged 16 to 22 Years." *The Journal of the American Medical Association, 219*(8), 1018–23.

Rosenau, P.M. (1992). *Post-Modernism and the Social Sciences: Insights, Inroads, and Intrusions.* Princeton, NJ: Princeton University Press.

Rule, J. (2001, Spring). "The Heterosexual Cage of Coupledom." *BC Bookworld.* Retrieved October 29, 2008, from <abcbookworld.com/view_essay.php?id=38>.

Rutter, P. (2007). "Young Adult Suicide and Sexual Orientation: What Should Counselors Know?" *Journal of LGBT Issues in Counseling, 1*(3), 33–48.

Saewyc, E.M., C. Poon, Y. Homma, and C. Skay. (2008). "Stigma Management? The Link Between Enacted Stigma and Teen Pregnancy Trends among Gay, Lesbian, and Bisexual Students in British Columbia." *The Canadian Journal of Human Sexuality, 17*(3), 123–39.

Saewyc, E.M., C. Poon, N. Wang, Y. Homma, A. Smith, and McCreary Centre Society. (2007). *Not Yet Equal: The Health of Lesbian, Gay and Bisexual Youth in BC.*

Vancouver, BC: McCreary Centre Society.

Saewyc, E.M, N. Wang, M. Chittenden, A. Murphy, and McCreary Centre Society. (2006). *Building Resilience in Vulnerable Youth.* Vancouver, BC: McCreary Centre Society.

Salerno, R. (2009, October 20). "Gay Man Murdered in Downtown Toronto." *Xtra!* Retrieved March 7, 2010, from <xtra.ca/public/Toronto/Gay_man_murdered_in_downtown_Toronto-7665.aspx>.

Samis, S. (1995) "'An Injury to One Is an Injury to All': Heterosexism, Homophobia, and Anti-Gay/Lesbian Violence in Greater Vancouver." Unpublished master's thesis, Department of Sociology and Anthropology, Simon Fraser University, Burnaby, BC.

Sausa, L. (2005). "Translating Research into Practice: Trans Youth Recommendations for Improving School Systems." *Journal of Gay and Lesbian Issues in Education,* 3(1), 15–28.

Savin-Williams, R. (1990). *Gay and Lesbian Youth: Expressions of Identity.* New York: Hemisphere Publication Corp.

———. (2005). *The New Gay Teenager.* Cambridge, MA: Harvard University Press.

Scholinski, D. (1997). *The Last Time I Wore a Dress: A Memoir.* New York: Riverhead Books.

"School System Accused of Same-Sex Discrimination." (2005, July 11). *CBCNews. ca.* Retrieved February 27, 2008, from <cbc.ca/canada/british-columbia/story/2005/07/11/bc_same-sex-teachers20050711.html>.

Schrader, A., and K. Wells. (2005). "Queer Perspectives on Social Responsibility in Canadian Schools and Libraries: Analysis and Resources. *School Libraries in Canada Online,* 24(4), 1–34.

Serano, J. (2007). *Whipping Girl: A Transsexual Woman on Sexism and the Scapegoating of Femininity.* Emeryville, CA: Seal Press.

Shariff, S (2008). *Cyber-Bullying: Issues and Solutions for the School, the Classroom, and the Home.* Oxfordshire, UK: Routledge.

Shelley, C. (2008). *Transpeople: Repudiation, Trauma, Healing.* Toronto, ON: University of Toronto Press.

Smith, A., E. Saewyc, L. MacKay, M. Northcott, and McCreary Centre Society. (2007). *Against the Odds: A Profile of Marginalized Street-Involved Youth in BC.* Vancouver, BC: McCreary Centre Society.

Smith, D. (2005). *Institutional Ethnography: A Sociology for People.* Lanham, MD: AltaMira Press.

Smith, D. (2009, May 15). "Siksay Tables Trans Bill for a Third Time." *Xtra.* Retrieved August 16, 2009, from <xtra.ca/public/National/Siksay_tables_trans_bill_for_a_third_time-6761.aspx>.

Smith, G. (1998). "The Ideology of 'Fag': The School Experience of Gay Students." *The Sociological Quarterly,* 39(2), 309–55.

Sokal, A. (2008). *Beyond the Hoax: Science, Philosophy and Culture.* Oxford, UK: Oxford University Press.

Steffenhagen, J. (2009, November 13). "Chilliwack Teachers Want Policies to Protect Gay, Lesbian, Bisexual Students." *Vancouver Sun.* Retrieved March 13, 2010, from <communities.canada.com/vancouversun/blogs/reportcard/archive/2009/11/13/homophobia.aspx>.

Stepp, L.S. (2001, June 19). "A Lesson in Cruelty: Anti-Gay Slurs Common at School." *Washington Post.* Retrieved July 11, 2010, from <encyclopedia.com/doc/1P2-446825.html>.

Stewart, W. (1995). *Cassell's Queer Companion: A Dictionary of Lesbian and Gay Life and Culture.* New York: Cassell.

Swartz, D. (1997). *Culture and Power: The Sociology of Pierre Bourdieu.* Chicago/London: University of Chicago Press.

Sykes, H. (2004) "Pedagogies of Censorship, Injury, and Masochism: Teacher Responses to Homophobic Speech in Physical Education. *Journal of Curriculum Studies, 36*(1), 75–99.

Szklarski, C. (2008, April 11). "Many Find Facebook a Negative Influence." *TheStar. com.* Retrieved November 7, 2008, from <thestar.com/News/Canada/article/413701>.

Tarun. (2007). "Heteronormativity in Educational Institutions." In N. Menon (Ed.), *Sexualities: Issues in Contemporary Indian Feminism* (pp. 128–40). New York: Zed Books.

Thompson, K. (2004). "Transsexuals, Transvestites, Transgender People, and Cross-Dressers." In. M. Stein (Ed.), *Encyclopedia of Lesbian, Gay, Bisexual, and Transgender History in America,* Vol. 3 (pp. 203–208). New York: Scribner's.

Tin, L.G. (Ed.). (2008/2003). *The Dictionary of Homophobia: A Global History of Gay and Lesbian Experience* (M. Redburn, A. Micahud and K. Mathers, Trans.). Vancouver, BC: Arsenal Pulp Press.

Trans Accessibility Project. (n.d.). "Transphobia and Discrimination." Retrieved November 6, 2008, from <queensu.ca/humanrights/tap/3discrimination.htm>.

Trans Youth: Information for Transgender Youth, their Service Providers, Friends, and Allies. (2003). *Trans Alliance Society.* Retrieved March 10, 2008, from <transalliancesociety.org/education/documents/03transyouth.pdf>.

Triangle Program. (n.d.). *Mission Statement.* Retrieved February 24, 2008, from <schools.tdsb.on.ca/triangle/mission.html>.

Valentine, G., R. Butler, and T. Skelton. (2001). "The Ethical and Methodological Complexities of Doing Research with 'Vulnerable' Young People." *Ethics, Place and Environment, 4*(2), 119–25.

Varjas, K., W. Mahan, J. Meyers, L. Birkbichler, and B. Dew. (2007). "Assessing School Climate among Sexual Minority High School Students." *Journal of LGBT Issues in Counselling, 1*(3), 49–75.

Vriend v. Alberta, [1998] 1 S.C.R. 493. Retrieved August 24, 2008, from <csc.lexum.umontreal.ca/en/1998/1998rcs1-493/1998rcs1-493.html>.

Walls, N.E. (2008). "Toward a Multidimensional Understanding of Heterosexism: The Changing Nature of Prejudice." *Journal of Homosexuality, 55*(1), 20–51.

Walton, G. 2004). "Bullying and Homophobia in Canadian Schools: The Politics of Policies, Programs and Educational Leadership." *Journal of Gay and Lesbian Issues in Education, 1*(4), 23–36.

———. (2006). "'No Fags Allowed': An Examination of Bullying as a Problematic and Implications for Educational Policy." Unpublished doctoral dissertation, Faculty of Education, Queen's University, Kingston, ON.

Warner, T. (2002). *Never Going Back: A History of Queer Activism in Canada.* Toronto, ON: University of Toronto Press.

Whittle, S., L. Turner, and M. Al-Alami. (2007). "Engendered Penalties: Transgender and Transsexual People's Experiences of Inequality and Discrimination." West Yorkshire, UK: The Equalities Review. Retrieved October 23, 2008, from <lluk.org/documents/engendered_penalties.pdf>.

Winfree, L., and H. Abadinsky. (2003). *Understanding Crime: Theory and Practice.* Belmont, CA: Wadsworth/Thomson Learning.

Wintonyk, D. (2008, September 28). "More Charges Possible For B.C. Gay Bashing Suspect." *CTV British Columbia.* Retrieved September 28, 2008, from <ctvbc.ctv.ca/servlet/an/local/CTVNews/20080929/BC_hate_crime_court_080929/200809 29/?hub=BritishColumbiaHome>.

Woolgar, S., and D. Pawluch. (1985). "Ontological Gerrymandering." *Social Problems, 32*(3), 214–27.

Wyss, S. (2004). "'This Was My Hell': The Violence Experienced by Gender Non-Conforming Youth in US High Schools." *International Journal of Qualitative Studies in Education, 17*(5), 709–30.

Youdell, D. (2004). "Wounds and Reinscriptions: Schools, Sexualities, and Performative Subjects." *Discourse: Studies in the Cultural Politics of Education, 25*(4), 477–93.